402

HUGO'S
GREEK
PHRASE BOOK

published by

Hugo's Language Books Limited
104 JUDD STREET, LONDON, W.C.1

FIRST PUBLISHED 1971

© 1971 Hugo's Language Books Ltd.

ISBN: 085285 023 9

Latest reprint 1976

*Facts and figures given in this book were
correct when printed. If you discover any
changes, please write to us.*

Printed in Great Britain by
THE ANCHOR PRESS LTD, TIPTREE, ESSEX

Contents

Contents

Introduction

This is primarily a phrase book in which selections of everyday words and phrases, complete with imitated pronunciation, are grouped under the usual headings of "Hotel", "Motoring", "Shopping" and so on. There are also conversion tables for weights, measures, distances, tyre pressures and clothing sizes.

In addition to the general notes that accompany each heading, there is more detailed information on Greek history, regions, social habits, traditional festivals, food and wine. It sometimes happens that the tourist, despite his excellent intentions, causes both himself and his host unnecessary embarrassment by committing some innocent breach of local custom or etiquette. We hope that this book will enable you to avoid making such mistakes, as well as helping you to make yourself understood.

The Language, Imitated Pronunciation

This book is no place in which to explain the intricacies of Greek grammar, but it will bear a few simple explanations to show why there are so many different word endings, even if you cannot use these yourself. Your wishes will in most cases be understood, despite everything!

The following Greek letters and letter combinations are pronounced in one way only, and should give you no trouble (in each case, the small letter follows the capital):

A, α: *a* as in "man"
B, β: *v* as in "very"
Δ, δ: *th* as in "there"
E, ε; AI, αι: *e* as in "pen"

Z, ζ: *z* as in "zest"
H, η; I, ι; Y, υ; EI, ει;
  OI, οι: *i* as in "pin"
Θ, θ: *th* as in "theatre"

Λ, λ: *l* as in "love"	Ψ, ψ: *ps* as in "upstairs"
M, μ: *m* as in "mouse"	OY, ου: *oo* as in "book"
N, ν: *n* as in "no"	ΜΠ, μπ: *b* as in "boy"
Ξ, ξ: *ks* as in "books"	NT, ντ: *d* as in "day"
O, o; Ω, ω: *o* as in "hot"	ΓΓ, γγ: *ng* as in "longer"
Π, π: *p* as in "pan"	ΓΚ, γκ: *ng* as in "longer"
P ρ: *r* as in "Rome"	ΓΧ, γχ: *n* and *h* run
T, τ: *t* as in "time"	together—almost
Φ, φ: *f* as in "festival"	a *j* sound

Ones which have variable forms of pronunciation are:

Γ, γ: Almost an *r* as in the French "roi"—a rolled guttural *gh* at the back of the throat. But before ι, η, υ, ει, οι: as "ye" (a long *e*). Before ε or αι: as *ye* in "yet" (a short *e*).

Κ, κ: *k* as in "kite". But before ι, η, υ, ει, οι: as "ye" preceded by *k* (*k'ye*). Before ε or αι: as *ye* in "yet" preceded by *k* (*k'yeh*).

Σ, σ: *s* as in "sample". But before μ, β, ρ, γ: *z* as in "zest".

Χ, χ: *h* as in "hot", although more guttural. But before ι, η, υ, ει, οι: as "ye" preceded by *h* (*h'ye*). Before ε or αι: as *ye* in "yet" preceded by *h* (*h'yeh*).

AY, αυ: *av* as in "have" when before γ, λ, μ, ν, ρ, o, ω. Otherwise as *af* in "café".

EY, ευ: *ev* as in "ever" when before γ, λ, μ, ν, ρ, o, ω. Otherwise as *ef* in "effort".

In the imitated pronunciation the sound of Δ, δ is represented by *th* in bold type; this **must** be pronounced as in "there" or "the". Where *th* is not in bold type it represents Θ, θ and should be pronounced as in "theatre", "thin". Similarly, where the sound of Χ, χ is guttural, like *ch* in the Scottish "loch" (not "lock"), we show it as *H* (it is best to pronounce this letter thus on all occasions). The guttural gamma (Γ, γ) is imitated by *gh*.

There are three accents in printed Greek (ά, ὰ, ᾶ) and it is important to place the stress on the right syllable. This is marked by a ′ in our imitated pronunciation. Do not confuse the Greek accents with those little commas (called "breathings") which are placed over some letters—these can be ignored. Do not hurry; deliberate and clear speech will greatly improve your chances of being understood. Keep all vowel sounds pure; the frequent appearance of an *h* in the imitated pronunciation, especially after *o*, is intended to ensure this. Syllables such as *–toh–* and *–noh–* might otherwise be wrongly pronounced to rhyme with the English words "to" and "no", if the *h* were to be omitted. Remember: *o* is as in "hot", not as in "go".

In modern spoken (demotic) Greek the article, noun and adjective are all inflected—they agree in number, gender and case. There are two numbers (singular and plural), three genders (masculine, feminine and neuter) and three cases (nominative or subject, genitive or possessive, and accusative or object).

The definite article "the" is declined thus:

SINGULAR	*Masculine*	*Feminine*	*Neuter*
Nom.: the	ὁ (*oh*)	ἡ (*ee*)	τό (*toh*)
Gen.: of the	τοῦ (*too*)	τῆς (*tiss*)	τοῦ (*too*)
Acc.: the	τόν (*ton*)	τήν (*tin*)	τό (*toh*)

PLURAL			
Nom.: the	οἱ (*ee*)	οἱ (*ee*)	τά (*tah*)
Gen.: of the	τῶν (*ton*)	τῶν (*ton*)	τῶν (*ton*)
Acc.: the	τούς (*toos*)	τίς (*tiss*)	τά (*tah*)

The indefinite article "a" is declined thus:

	Masculine	*Feminine*	*Neuter*
Nom.: a (an)	ἕνας (*en' nahs*)	μιά (*me-ah'*)	ἕνα (*en'-nah*)
Gen.: of a (an)	ἑνός (*en-noss'*)	μιᾶς (*me-ahs'*)	ἑνός (*en-noss'*)
Acc.: a (an)	ἕνα (*en'-nah*)	μιά (*me-ah'*)	ἕνα (*en'-nah*)

Note that in the word lists, where an adjective occurs, we give the masculine, feminine and neuter singular, and underneath come the plural forms for each gender. Where it is necessary we have put the Greek "the" in brackets before the noun, thus enabling you to identify the gender at once.

A Brief Background to Greece

Covering an area of about 51,000 square miles, with a population of some 8¾ million, Greece can most conveniently be divided into mainland peninsula and islands (some 1400 of them). The mainland has more than 9,000 miles of extremely indented coastline and is generally rugged and mountainous. The highest point is that legendary home of the gods, Mount Olympus, at 9,569 feet. Tucked in behind and among the mountains are beautiful valleys and plains which cradle remains of the ancient glory of Greece. The southern half of the mainland, the Peloponnese, is almost an island; this large peninsula is joined to central Greece by a narrow isthmus at Corinth. The Corinth canal (first thought of by the Roman emperor Nero) was eventually cut between 1882 and 1893. Including the port of Piraeus and suburbs, the capital city of Athens has a population of just under two million; the second city is Thessaloniki (Salonika), in the northern province of Macedonia.

The islands, most of which are uninhabited, are in several groups. Off the west coast lie the Ionian Islands; these include Corfu and Ithaca (the legendary home of Odysseus). The Cyclades and the Dodecanese occupy the southern Aegean and embrace such magnificent tourist centres as Rhodes, Mykonos, Delos and Naxos. Crete, the largest Greek island, lies further south. Another large island, Euboea, is off the mainland's eastern shore, with the Northern Sporades close by. More islands are off the Turkish coast and in the northern Aegean.

11

Climate. As might be expected, Greece has a mild Mediterranean-type climate, with an average of 300 sunny days per year in the southern half of the country. This has a mean summer temperature of around 80°F (26·7°C), in winter around 50°F (10°C). Although mid-summer temperatures can top 100°F (37·8°C), it is a dry heat and therefore not as oppressive as in places with greater humidity. Added to which, there is often a slight sea breeze to help cool you. The north is not quite so hot in summer, and winter temperatures are much lower.

The country is at its best during spring (early March to the beginning of May) and autumn (end of September to late November). Rainfall is highest on the west coast; Corfu, the greenest place in Greece, is alone in having a climate comparable to that of Western Europe. Athens is particularly dry, with only brief winter showers to interrupt the sunshine, and Crete is top of the sunshine league.

History. With some 4,000 years of history behind it, Greece can justly claim to be the cradle of Western civilisation. The legends of the gods and mythological heroes such as Hercules and Agamemnon are rooted in dateless years long before the Mycenaean supremacy of the 13th century BC; kings came and kings went, and we must thank the poet Homer for much of what we now accept as facts concerning this period. From the tenth to the first century BC the classical era ran its course; a tribe or city would rise to political, military and intellectual supremacy, only to go down before another or commit suicide after casting out its hero in a fashion that is exemplified in Greek dramatic tragedy.

Alexander the Great's empire reached as far as India, but after his death in 323 BC there came another decline which led eventually to the Roman occupation of Greece. In the 4th century AD, when the Roman empire was split into western and eastern halves, Greece belonged to the latter. The Byzantine rulers began to plunder; Huns and Goths, with other barbarian tribes, followed suit and years of strife ensued. The Crusaders' victories over the Byzantine empire gave the country a brief respite, albeit still under foreign domination, but soon the Turks were back in power. Their absolute domination and exploitation of the people, which lasted until the early 19th century, was cruel in the extreme and it accounts for the ill-feeling which Greeks still have towards Turks.

Britain, France and Russia, appreciating the strategic value of the Balkans and wishing to contain the Turks, combined to free southern Greece from her oppressors. By the end of the 19th century, after further risings, bloodshed and political wrangling, the Turks had gone altogether from Greek territory. Indeed, after the 1st World War Greece occupied parts of Turkey; these areas were returned in 1923, and a huge number of Greeks had to be repatriated as a result—placing a strain on the national economy which was none too healthy in the first place. Ever since then the country has never really settled down; there were a few progressive years after the civil war of 1949, but the Cyprus problem sparked off more trouble and resignations, and political uncertainty still exists.

Social Habits and Customs

The Greeks are a quite different people from those of other Mediterranean countries. They are a little less voluble and exuberant, and are milder in both speech and manner. Their traditional hospitality is genuine and spontaneous (the word for both "stranger" and "guest" is "xenos"), and they are also forthright and emotional. A Greek needs little encouragement to speak to a stranger, and he will go out of his way to help a visitor. They are a race of travellers themselves, having since their earliest days journeyed to far-off places in search of fame and fortune. There are few villages in Greece where some of the inhabitants have not spent a part of their lives in the United States and other foreign countries; while they are abroad they send money back to their families in order to keep aged parents or other relatives in comfort, or to ensure that their sisters have an adequate dowry upon getting married. The Greek's natural eagerness to help, coupled with his adeptness at learning a foreign language, has given great relief to many a visitor whose knowledge of Greek is next to nothing. The natives of the islands are particularly affable and possess a fine sense of form, colour and harmony which is immediately apparent in the architecture and decoration of most homes.

It is hardly surprising that the Greeks do not like being reminded of all those years they spent under Turkish rule, and as a result you will hear Turkish coffee referred to as Greek coffee. As a sign of their hospitality you will be given a glass of water, some Turkish Delight or a spoonful of jam, and a cup of Greek coffee. To please your host, first eat the sweet, then drink the water and follow with the coffee. If you have any occasion to repay some hospitality, present your host with the little gift of a "komboloi". This is similar to a rosary and the beads are usually made of amber. A Greek always has one handy to play with while indulging in the national pastime of deep and secret contemplation.

The usual forms of address (Mr, Mrs and Miss) are, respectively, Κύριε, Κυρία, Δεσποινίς (pronounced: *kir'-re-eh, kir-ree'-ah, thess-pin-ees'*). When referring to someone else, or introducing yourself, say ὁ Κύριος, ἡ Κυρία, ἡ Δεσποινίς (*oh kir'-re-oss, ee kir-ree'-ah, ee thess-pin-ees'*); this change represents the article taking the nominative or subject case. Upon being introduced, say "Χαίρω πολύ" (*Hair'-oh poh-lee'*, "how do you do"), and take your leave by saying "Χάρηκα πολύ" (*Hah'-re-kah poh-lee'*, "pleased to have met you"). The general expression for both greeting and leave-taking is Χαίρετε (*Hair'-eh-teh*), but a more specific form of welcoming expression is Καλῶς ἤρθατε or Καλῶς ὡρίσατε (*kah-loss' eer'-thah-teh* or *kah-loss' oh-ree'-sah-teh*, literally, "Welcome, you've arrived") to which you should reply "Καλῶς σᾶς ηὕραμε" (*kah-loss' sahs ee'-vrah-meh*, "Welcome, I've found you").

The Greeks have a number of other expressions for use on various occasions, but the average tourist will be unlikely to need to use these. When a Greek shakes his head from side to side and says nothing he means "I don't know". If, at the same time, he says *o'-H'ye* he means "no". If he nods downwards and says nothing or *neh, neh*, he means "yes". If he nods upwards and says nothing or

15

o'-H'ye he means "no". Never hold out your hand with the fingers wide-spread; if you do, you may find yourself in trouble. It means "curse you".

Like the citizens of present-day Rome, they think of themselves as a modern society and don't appear to concern themselves with the glory that *was* Greece; this is left to the official guides. They will like you more if you restrain your eulogies on Ancient Greece until you return home. Your native friends will be much more impressed.

Greeks, with odd exceptions, are not heavy drinkers and it is not automatically expected of you to take wine with your meals. If you drink water, no eyebrows will be raised. Conversely, you are expected to eat something, be it only a snack, if you drop into a taverna or cafe for a drink. This is not an attempt to make you part with your money, but customary practice—see how many of the locals do it, and how few are drunk as a result. When you want the waiter, clap your hands; this is the usual method and you will not be considered rude. Unpunctuality is not a crime; indeed, to be on time in summer would be exceptional. The siesta is still preserved as a national custom in the summer months and it is unheard of to disturb anybody between 2 pm and 5 pm.

Finally, resist the temptation to flirt with the pretty girls, particularly in Crete; it is more than likely that a jealous and fiery lover or husband, a father or a brother, is close by!

Useful Everyday Words and Phrase

about (=approx.) περίπου *pair-ee'-poo*
about (=concerning) γιά *yah*

above ἐπάνω *eh-pan'-o*
across ἀπέναντι *ah-pen'-an-de*
after ἔπειτα *eh'-pe-ta*
again πάλιν *pa'-leen*
at εἰς *iss*
before (= of time) πρίν *prrin*
before (= of place) ἐμπρός *em-bross'*
behind ὀπίσω *op-ee'-so*
beneath ἀποκάτω *ah-poh-ka'-toh*
between μεταξύ *meh-tax-eé*
big μεγάλος,μεγάλη,μεγάλο
    meh-ghal'-oss,meh-ghal'-e,meh-ghal'-oh
    μεγάλοι,μεγάλες,μεγάλα
    meh-ghal'-e,meh-ghal'-ess,meh-ghal'-ah
by πλησίον,κοντά,μέ *ple-sse'-on,kon-dah',meh*
cold κρύος,κρύα,κρύο *kree'-oss,kree'-ah,kree'-o*
    κρύοι,κρύες,κρύα *kree'-e,kree'-ess,kree'-a*
down κάτω *kah'-to*
drink (*v.*) πίνω *pee'-noh*
drink (*n.*) (τό) ποτό *poh-toh'*
enough ἀρκετά *arrk-yeh-tah'*
everybody ὅλοι *orl'-ee*
everything ὅλα *orl'-ah*
everywhere παντού *pan-doo'*
far μακρυά *mahk-ree-ah'*
fast γρήγορα *ghree'-ghor-ah*
food (ἡ) τροφή *trof-ee'*
good καλός,καλή,καλό *kah-loss',kah-lee',kah-lo'*
    καλοί,καλές,καλά *kah-lee',kah-less',kah-lah'*
here ἐδῶ *eh-thoh'*
high ὑψηλά *ips-e-lah'*

how πῶς *poss*
in εἰς *iss*
inside μέσα *mess'-ah*
left ἀριστερά *ah-rees-tair-rah'*
less ὀλιγώτερο *ol-lee-ghot'-air-o*
like καθώς,ὅπως,σάν *kah-thos',op'-oss,sun*
little (*adv.*) λίγο *lee'-gho*
little (*adj.*) μικρός,μικρή,μικρό
             me-kross',me-kree',me-kroh'
             μικροί,μικρές,μικρά
             me-kree',me-kress',me-krah'
lost χαμένο *Hah-men'-oh*
many πολλοί,πολλές,πολλά *poll-y',poll-ess',poll-ah'*
mine δικός μου,δική μου,δικό μου
             the-koss' muh,the-kee' muh,the-koh muh
             δικοί μου,δικές μου,δικά μου
             the-kee' muh,the-kess' muh,the-kah' muh
more περισσότερο *pair-e-sot'-tair-o*
no ὄχι *o'-H'ye*
near ἀκούω *ah-koo'-oh*
open ἀνοιχτός,ἀνοιχτή,ἀνοιχτό
             ah-nich-toss',ah-nich-tee',ah-nich-toh'
             ἀνοιχτοί,ἀνοιχτές,ἀνοιχτά
             ah-nich-tee',ah-nich-tess',ah-nich-tah'
please παρακαλῶ *pah-rah-kah-lo'*
right δεξιά *theck-see-ah'*
somebody κάποιος,κάποια,κάποιο
             kap'-ee-oss,kap'-ee-ah,kap'-ee-oh
             κάποιοι,κάποιες,κάποια
             kap'-ee-ee,kap'-ee-ess,kap'-ee-ah
something κάτι *kat'-ty*

thank you εὐχαριστῶ *ef-Hah-re-stoh'*
there ἐκεῖ *eh-kee'*
this αὐτός,αὐτή,αὐτό *ahf-toss',ahf-tee',ahf-toh'*
those ἐκεῖνοι,ἐκεῖνες,ἐκεῖνα
   eck-ee'-nee,eck-ee'-ness,eck-ee'-nah
through μέσῳ *mess'-oh*
too ἐπίσης *eh-pee'-siss*
under κάτω *kah'-toh*
until μέχρι,ἕως *meH'-ree,ay'-oss*
up ἐπάνω *eh-pan'-o*
very πολύ *poh-lee'*
when ὅταν *ot'-an*
where ποῦ *puh*
why γιατί *yat-ee'*
without δίχως,χωρίς *the'-Hoss,Hor-reece'*
yes ναί,μάλιστα *neh,mah'-lees-tah*

USEFUL EVERYDAY PHRASES

Could you direct me to . . .? Μπορεῖτε νά μοῦ πῆτε ποῦ
   εἶναι ὁ . . ἡ . . τό
   boh-re'-teh nah mou pe'-teh pou ee'-neh . . .
   oh . . . ee . . . toh
Do you speak English? Ὁμιλεῖτε Ἀγγλικά;
   oh-me-lee'-teh ahn-gle-kah'
Go away! φύγε
   fee'-yeh
Have you a list of Ἔχετε κατάλογο
excursions? ἐκδρομῶν;
   ay'-Heh-teh kat-ah'-logh-o ek-thro-mon'
Have you anything cheaper? Ἔχετε τίποτα φθηνότερο;
   ay'-Heh-teh te'-poh-ta ef-the-not'-air-o

19

How are you?	Πῶς εἶσθε;
	poss ees'-theh
How long does it take to …?	πόσην ὥρα παίρνει γιά …;
	poss'-in or'-ah pair'-ne ya …
How much is it?	πόσο στοιχίζει;
	poss'-oh ste-Hee'-ze
I am an Englishman	Εἶμαι Ἄγγλος
	ee'-meh ahn'-glos
I am an Englishwoman	Εἶμαι Ἀγγλίδα
	ee'-meh ahn-glee'-tha
I am very sorry	Λυποῦμαι πάρα πολύ
	le-poo'-meh pah'-rah pol-lee'
I cannot speak Greek	Δέν ξέρω Ἑλληνικά
	then ksair'-o el-le-ne-ka'
I do not wish to speak to you	Δέν ἐπιθυμῶ νά σοῦ μιλήσω
	then ep-pe-thee-moh' nah soo me-lee'-soh
I do not understand	Δέν καταλαβαίνω
	then kah-tah-lah-ven'-oh
I enjoyed myself immensely	Ἐδιασκέδασα ὑπερβολικά
	eh-the-ahs-keh'-thah sah e-per-vol-e-kah'
I have lost my way	Ἔχασα τόν δρόμο
	eh'-Hah-sah ton thro'-moh
I have no time	Δέν ἔχω καιρό
	then eh'-Hoh keh-roh'
Is this enough?	Εἶναι αὐτό ἀρκετό;
	ee'-neh af-toh' ar-keh-toh'
It is very good	Εἶναι πάρα πολύ καλό
	ee'-neh pah'-rah pol-le' kah-loh'
Look!	Κύττα
	kee'-tah

Please write it down	Μοῦ τό γράφετε, παρακαλῶ;

mou toh ghrah'-fet-eh, pah-rah-kah-lo'

Thank you for your hospitality — Σᾶς εὐχαριστῶ γιά τήν φιλοξενία σας

sahss ef-Hah-re-stoh' yah tin fee-locks-en-ee'-ah sahss

This is incorrect — Αὐτό δέν εἶναι σωστό

af-toh' then ee'-neh soss-toh'

We are in a hurry — Βιαζόμεθα

vee-ah-zom'-eh-tha

What is that? — τί εἶναι ἐκεῖνο;

tee een'-eh eh-ke'-noh

What is the correct time? — Τί ὥρα εἶναι ἀκριβῶς;

tee or'ah een'-eh ah-kree voss'

Where can I get a . . .? — Πού μπορῶ νά εὕρω . . .;

poo bor-roh' nah ev'-roh

Would you please speak slowly? — Μιλᾶτε παρακαλῶ σιγά;

me-lah'-teh pah-rah-kah-lo' see-ghah'

Your good health — Εἰς ὑγείαν

ees ee-ghee'-an

Good morning, good evening — Καλημέρα, Καλησπέρα

kah-le-meh'-rah, kah-lis-peh'-rah

Hullo *or* goodbye — Χαίρετε

Hair'-eh-teh

DAYS OF THE WEEK, MONTHS AND SEASONS

Sunday Κυριακή *kirry-ah-kee'*
Monday Δευτέρα *thef-teh'-rah*
Tuesday Τρίτη *tree'-te*
Wednesday Τετάρτη *teh-tar'-te*

Thursday Πέμπτη *pemp'-te*
Friday Παρασκευή *pah-rah-skeh-vee'*
Saturday Σάββατο *sah'vah-to*

January 'Ιανουάριος *yan-oo-are'-e-oss*
February Φεβρουάριος *fev-roo-ah'-re-oss*
March Μάρτιος *mar'-te-oss*
April 'Απρίλιος *ah-pree'-le-oss*
May Μάϊος *my'-oss*
June 'Ιούνιος *ee-oo'-ne-oss*
July 'Ιούλιος *ee-oo'-le-oss*
August Αΰγουστος *av'-ghoos-toss*
September Σεπτέμβριος *sep-tem'-vre-oss*
October 'Οκτώβριος *ock-tov'-re-oss*
November Νοέμβριος *no-em'-vre-oss*
December Δεκέμβριος *theck-em'-vre-oss*

Spring (ἡ)ἄνοιξι *an'-ick-se*
Summer (τό)καλοκαίρι *kah-lo-keh'-ree*
Autumn (τό)φθινόπωρο *fthin-op'-oh-roh*
Winter (ὁ)χειμώνας *Him-on'-ass*

NUMBERS

1	ἕνα *en'-ah*	**5**	πέντε *pen'-deh*
2	δύο *the'-o*	**6**	ἕξι *ex'-see*
3	τρία *tree'-ah*	**7**	ἑπτά *ep-tah'*
4	τέσσερα *tess'-er-rah*	**8**	ὀκτώ *ock-toh'*

9 ἐννέα
en-neh'-ah

10 δέκα
theck'-ah

11 ἕνδεκα
en'-theck-ah

12 δώδεκα
tho'-theck-ah

13 δέκα τρία
theck'-ah tree'-ah

14 δέκα τέσσερα
theck'-ah tess'-er'rah

15 δέκα πέντε
theck'-ah pen'-deh

16 δέκα ἕξι
theck'-ah ex'-see

17 δέκα ἑπτά
theck'-ah ep-tah'

18 δέκαζοκτώ
theck'ah ock-toh'

19 δέκα ἐννέα
theck'-ah en-neh'-ah

20 εἴκοσι
ee'-kos'see

21 εἴκοσι ἕνα
ee'-kos-see en'-nah

22 εἴκοσι δύο
ee'-kos-see the'-o

23 εἴκοσι τρία
ee'-kos-see tree'-ah

30 τριάντα
tre-ahn'-dah

40 σαράντα
sah-rahn'-dah

50 πενῆντα
pen-een'-dah

60 ἑξῆντα
ex-een'-dah

70 ἑβδομήντα
ev-thoh-meen'-dah

80 ὀγδόντα
ogh-thon'-dah

90 ἐννενήντα
en-en-een'-dah

100 ἑκατό
eck-ah-toh'

200 διακόσια
the-ah-kos'-sah

1000 χίλια
Heel'-ya

2000 δύο χιλιάδες
the'-oh Heel-e-ah'-thess

¼ ἕνα τέταρτο
en'-nah teh'-tar-to

½ μισό
mee-soh'

¾ τρία τέταρτα
tree'-ah teh'-tar-tah

⅓ ἕνα τρίτο
en'-nah tree'-toh

1st πρῶτος, πρώτη, πρῶτο
proh'-tos, proh'-tee, proh'-toh
2nd δεύτερος, δεύτερη, δεύτερο
thef'-teh-ros, thef'-teh-ree, thef'-teh-roh
3rd τρίτος, τρίτη, τρίτο
tree'-tos, tree'-te, tree'-toh

TIME

today σήμερα *see'-meh-rah*
yesterday χθές *Hthess*
tomorrow αὔριο *av'-ree-oh*
last year πέρυσι *pair'-ee-see*
this morning σήμερα τό πρωΐ *see'-meh-rah toh proh-ee*
this afternoon σήμερα τό ἀπόγευμα
see'-meh-rah toh ah-poh'-yev-mah
this evening ἀπόψε *ahp-op'-seh*
last night χθές τήν νύκτα *Hthess tin nick'-tah*
tomorrow night αὔριο τήν νύκτα *av'-ree-oh tin nick'-tah*
tomorrow evening αὔριο τό βράδι
av'-ree-oh toh vrah'-thee
next week τήν ἐρχόμενη ἑβδομάδα
tin air-Hom'-en-ee ev-tho-mah'-tha
last week τήν περασμένη ἑβδομάδα
tin pair-as-men'-ee ev-tho-mah'-tha
minute (τό) λεπτό *lep-toh'*
hour (ή) ὥρα *or'-rah*
day (ή) ἡμέρα *ee-mair'-ah*
fortnight (τό) δεκαπενθήμερο *theck-ah-pen-the'-meh-roh*
month (ὁ) μήνας *mee'-nas*
next year τοῦ χρόνου *too Hron'-oo*

early ἐνωρίς *en-or-eece*
late ἀργά *ar-gha'*
one o'clock ἡ ὥρα μία *ee or'-rah mee'-ah*
quarter past one μία καὶ τέταρτο *mee'-ah keh teh'-tar-toh*
half past one μιάμισυ *me'-ah'-me-se*
quarter to two δύο παρά τέταρτο
                   the'-oh pah-rah' teh'-tar-toh
two o'clock ἡ ὥρα δύο *ee or'-rah the'-oh*
three o'clock ἡ ὥρα τρεῖς *ee or'-rah treece*
twelve o'clock ἡ ὥρα δώδεκα *ee or'-rah tho'-theck-ah*
noon μεσημέρι *mess-e-mair'-ee*
midnight μεσάνυκτα *mess-ah'-nick-tah*

COLOURS

black μαῦρο *mah'-vroh*
white ἄσπρο *ahs'-proh*
red κόκκινο *cok'-key-noh*
orange πορτοκαλλί *por-toh-kal-lee'*
yellow κίτρινο *kit'-tree-noh*
green πράσινο *prass'-ee-noh*
blue μπλέ *bleh*
indigo λουλακί *loo-lah-kee'*
violet βιολετί *ve-oh-let-ee'*
brown καφφετί *kaf-fet-ee'*
grey γκρίζο, σταχτί *gree'-zo, staH-tee'*
beige μπέζ *behz*
pink τριανταφυλλί, ρόζ *tre-ah-da-feel-ee', roz*
mauve μόβ *mohv*
purple πορφυρό *por-fe-roh'*
dark σκοῦρο *skoo'-roh*
light ἀνοιχτό *ah-niH-toh'*

PUBLIC NOTICES

Public notices are for the most part written in Greek (but see note under "Motoring" for road signs), and some of the more common ones are given below:

Bathroom	ΝΙΠΤΗΡΕΣ
Bus stop	ΣΤΑΣΙΣ ΛΕΩΦΟΡΕΙΟΥ
Cafe	ΚΑΦΕΝΕΙΟΝ
Chemist	ΦΑΡΜΑΚΕΙΟΝ
Closed	ΚΛΕΙΣΤΟΝ
Cold (water)	ΚΡΥΟΝ
Danger	ΚΙΝΔΥΝΟΣ
Entry	ΕΙΣΟΔΟΣ
Exit	ΕΞΟΔΟΣ
Free (vacant)	ΕΛΕΥΘΕΡΟΝ
Garage	ΓΚΑΡΑΖ
Gentlemen	ΑΝΔΡΕΣ
Hot (water)	ΖΕΣΤΟΝ
Information	ΠΛΗΡΟΦΟΡΙΑΙ
Ladies	ΓΥΝΑΙΚΕΣ
Lavatory	W.C.
Open	ΑΝΟΙΚΤΟΝ
Parking	ΣΤΑΘΜΕΥΣΙΣ ΑΤΥΟΚΙΝΗΤΩΝ
Post Office	ΤΑΧΥΔΡΟΜΕΙΟΝ
Pull	ΣΥΡΑΤΕ
Push	ΩΘΗΣΑΤΕ
Stop	ΣΤΑΣΙΣ

Accommodation

The hotels are classified into six categories; De Luxe or AA, and 1st to 5th Class or A to E.

AA De Luxe: Every room has a private bathroom, hot and cold running water, telephone and central heating. The staff speak foreign languages. Laundry service provided.

A 1st Class: Every room has private bath or shower, hot and cold running water, central heating and telephone. Staff speak foreign languages. Laundry service provided.

B 2nd Class: At least half the rooms have private bath or shower; every room has hot and cold water. Most rooms have telephone and central heating. Staff should speak one foreign language.

C 3rd Class: Private bathrooms are not compulsory (although in all new C Class hotels most of the rooms do have private showers). There is a W.C. to every 6 rooms, with central heating and hot and cold water in every room.

D 4th Class and E 5th Class: Hot running water is not compulsory; there must be one shower and W.C. to every 8 rooms, and cold running water in every room.

Of course, with the ever-increasing demands of tourists and the rapid rate in which hotels are appearing all over the country, there is bound to be some overlapping as far as the standards quoted above are concerned. Many of the National Tourist Organisation's new "Xenia" hotels, classified A and B, have better facilities than older establishments, and one can always find a seedy A Class place that is no better than an unpretentious C hotel.

It is wise to watch the various surcharges. In most hotels a 15% service charge is added to your bill, though this can be higher. A small extra charge is usually made for central heating and air conditioning in AA and A Class hotels. Few places offer garage space, although arrangements can often be made to park cars in nearby public garages.

The National Tourist Organisation of Greece publishes useful information on hotels which you may obtain from your travel agent or direct from N.T.O.G., 195–7 Regent Street, London W.1.

The Village Guest House

These enable visitors to enjoy the charm of Greek country life in the most picturesque villages, perched on mountain slopes, in lovely valleys or down by the sea. A simple clean room in a private house, furnished with essential needs to ensure a pleasant stay, awaits every visitor. Many of these charming guest houses are located in Attica, but for full information apply to: Royal National Foundation's Tourist Information Office, 9 Philhellinon Street, Athens.

Summer Holiday Camps

Since the founding of the Club Mediterrannée camp at Ipsos, on Corfu, the promotion of summer holiday camps has gained considerable impetus throughout the country in recent years. Camps are now located at various attractive seaside resorts in Attica, with accommodation in the form of bungalows, tents or (in some cases) permanent buildings. Amenities usually include a fully equipped restaurant, bar, dance floor, showers, a private beach and equipment for sea sports. The N.T.O.G. will supply an up-to-date list of addresses with the facilities available.

USEFUL WORDS AND PHRASES

basin (ὁ) νιπτήρ *nip-teer'*
bath (τό) μπάνιο *ban'-yo*
bathroom (ἡ) αἴθουσα λουτροῦ *eth'-oo-sah loo-troo'*
bed (τό) κρεββάτι *kreh-vah'-tee*
bedroom (ἡ) κρεββατοκάμαρα *kreh-vah-to-kam'-ah-rah*
(single) (μονή) *(mon-ee')*
(double) (διπλῆ) *(the-plee')*
bill (ὁ) λογαριασμός *lor-gha-ree-ahs-mos'*
blanket (ἡ) κουβέρτα *koo-vair'-tah*
board (full) δωμάτιο μέ ὅλα τά γεύματα
    tho-mah'-te-oh meh oh'-lah tah yev'-mah-tah
board (half) δωμάτιο μέ πρόγευμα
    tho-mah'-te-oh meh proh'-yev-mah
chair (ἡ) καρchair (ἡ) καρέκλα *kah-reck'-lah*
chambermaid (ἡ) καμαριέρα *kah-mar-yair'-ah*
coat-hanger (τό) κρεμαστάρι *kreh-mas-tar'-ee*
dining room (ἡ) τραπεζαρία *tra-pez-ah-ree'-ah*
eiderdown (τό) πάπλωμα *pahp'-lo-mah*
hotel (τό) ξενοδοχεῖο *kseh-noh-tho-Hee'-oh*
hot water bottle (ἡ) μπουγιώτα *boo-yot'-ah*

29

key (τό) κλειδ) *klee-the'*

lavatory (ή) τουαλέττα *too-ah-let'-tah*

lift (τό) ἀσανσέρ *or* (ὁ) ἀνελκυστήρ
    ah-sen-serr' or ah-nel-kiss-teer'

manager (ὁ) διευθυντής *the-ef-thin-diss'*

mattress (τό) στρῶμα *stro'-mah*

page boy (ὁ) ὑπηρέτης *ee-pee-ret'-iss*

pillow (τό) μαξιλάρι *max-il-ar'-e*

porter (ὁ) χαμάλης *Ha-mah'-liss*

proprietor (ὁ) ἰδιοκτήτης *ee-the-ock-tee'-tiss*

radiator (τό) καλοριφέρ *kah-lo-ree-fair'*

reading lamp (ή) λάμπα κομοδίνου
        lam'-bah koh-moh-the'-nuh

sheet (τό) σεντόνι *sen-don'-ee*

shutters (τά) παραθυρόφυλλα *or* (τά) παντζούρια
      pah-rah-the-rof'-feel-ah or *pahnd-zoor'-ee-ah*

soap (τό) σαπούνι *sah-po'-nee*

switch (τό) ἠλεκτρικό κουμπί *ee-leck-tre-ko' koom-bee'*

table (τό) τραπέζι *tra-pez'-ee*

tap (ή) βρύση *vree'-see*

  (cold water) κρύου νεροῦ *kree'-oo neh-roo'*

  (hot water) ζεστοῦ νεροῦ *zes-too' neh-roo'*

towel (ή) πετσέτα *pet-set-ah*

wardrobe (ή) ντουλάπα *doo-lah-pah*

window (τό) παράθυρο *pah-rah'-the-roh*

I am Mr (Mrs)	Εἶμαι ὁ κύριος (ἡ κυρία)
ee'-meh o keer'-re-oss (ee kee-ree'-ah)	
Have you a room for one night?	Ἔχετε δωμάτιο γιά μία νύχτα;
eh'-Heh-teh tho-mah'-te-oh yah me'-ah nick'-tah	

I wish to stay . . . days (1 week, 2 weeks)	Θέλω νά μείνω . . . ἥμερες (μία ἑβδομάδα, δύο ἑβ- δομάδες)

thel'-oh nah mee'-noh . . . e-mair'-ess (mee'-ah
ev-tho-mah'-thah, the'-oh ev-tho-mah'-thess

May I see the room?	Μοῦ δείχνετε τό δωμάτιο;

mou thiH'-neh-teh toh tho-mah'-te-oh

I want a room for myself only	Θέλω δωμάτιο γιά τόν ἐαυτό μου

thel'-oh tho-mah'-te-oh mon'-oh yah ton
ay-af-toh'-mou

Have you a room with a private bathroom?	Ἔχετε δωμάτιο μέ ἰδιαίτερο λουτρό;

eh'-Heh-teh tho-mah'-te-oh meh e-the-et'-air-o
loo-troh'

Any room will do	Οἰοδήποτε δωμάτιο μοῦ κάνει

e-oh-thee'-pot-eh tho-mah'-te-oh mou
kah'-ne

It is too noisy	Κάνει πολύ θόρυβο ἐδῶ

kah'-ne pol-lee' thor'-re-voh eh-thoh'

Can I overlook the sea (the garden)?	Ἔχετε δωμάτιο πού νά βλέπη στή θάλασσα; (στόν κήπο);

eh'-Heh-teh tho-mah'-te-oh pou nah vlep'-e ste
thah'-lahss-ah (ston kee'-poh)

Where is the bathroom?	Ποῦ εἶναι τό δωμάτιον λουτροῦ;

pou ee'-neh toh tho-mah'-te-oh loo-troo'

I only require breakfast	Θέλω πρόγευμα μόνον

thel'-oh proh'-yev-mah mon'-on

31

May I have breakfast in my room?	Μπορεῖτε νά μοῦ σερβίρετε τό πρόγευμα στό δωμάτιό μου;

boh-ree'-teh nah mou sair-vee'-reh-teh toh proh'-yer-mah stoh tho-mah-te-oh'-mou

I require breakfast and an evening meal	Θέλω πρόγευμα καί δεῖπνο

thel'-oh proh'-yev-mah keh theep'-noh

I require full board	Θέλω δωμάτιο μέ ὅλα τά γεύματα

thel'-oh tho-mah'-te-oh meh ol'-la tah yev'-ma-ta

Does that include all services and taxes?	Συμπεριλαμβάνονται ὅλες οἱ ἐξυπηρετήσεις καί οἱ φόροι;

seem-pair-e-lam-van'-on-deh oh'less ee ex-e-peer-et-ee'-sis keh ee for'-e

What do I do about laundry?	Ποῦ δίνονται τά ροῦχα γιά πλύσιμο;

pou the'- non-deh tah roo'-Hah yah plee'-se-moh

I want a pillow (a towel)?	Θέλω ἕνα μαξιλάρι (μιά πετσέτα)

thel'-oh en'-nah max-e-lah'-re (me-ah' pet-set'-ah)

May I have an extra blanket?	Μπορεῖτε νά μοῦ δώσετε ἀκόμη μία κουβέρτα;

boh-ree'-teh nah mou thoss'-eh-teh ah-kom'-e mee'-ah koo-vair'-tah

May I have a stronger light?	Μπορεῖτε νά μοῦ δώσετε πειό δυνατό γλόμπο;

boh-ree'-teh nah mou thoss'-eh-teh pe'oh' the-nah-toh'-ghlom'-boh

I am going to bed	πηγαίνω νά πλαγιάσω
	pe-yen'-oh nah plah-yah'-soh
Please call me at ...	Παρακαλῶ μέ ξυπνᾶτε στίς ...
	pah-rah-kah-loh' meh kseep-nah'-teh stees ...
I shall be back at ...	Θά ἐπιστρέψω στίς ...
	thah ep-e-strep'-so stees ...
Please open (close) the window	'Ανοίγετε (κλείνετε) τό παράθυρο
	ah-nee'-yet-eh (klee'-net-eh) toh pah-rah'-the-roh
I would like a hot bath	Θά ἤθελα νά κάνω ἕνα ζεστό λουτρό
	thah ee'-thel-ah nah kahn'-oh en'-nah zest-oh' loo-troh'
May I have some drinking water?	Θά ἤθελα ὀλίγο πόσιμο νερό
	thah ee'-thel-ah oh-lee'-gho poss'-e-moh neh-roh'
I need these clothes washed	Αὐτά τά ροῦχα πρέπει νά πλυθοῦν
	af-tah' tah roo'-Hah prep'-ee nah plee-thoon'
Can I have them back tomorrow?	Θά εἶναι ἕτοιμα αὔριο;
	thah ee'-neh et'-e-mah ahv'-re-oh
Would you repair this?	Μοῦ διορθώνετε αὐτό;
	mou the-or-thon'-eh-teh af-toh'
Would you dry these shoes (clothes) for me?	Μοῦ στεγνώνετε αὐτά τά παπούτσια (τά ροῦχα);
	mow stegh-non'-eh-teh af-tah' tah pah-poots'-e-ah (tah roo'-Hah)
What time do you close?	Τί ὥρα κλείνετε;
	tee or'-ah klee'-net-eh

C

May I have that table?	Μπορῶ νά ἔχω αὐτό τό τραπέζι;
	boh-roh' nah eh'-Ho af-toh' toh trah-pez'-ee
May I dine now?	Μπορῶ νά φάγω τώρα;
	boh-roh' nah fah'-gho tor'-ah
May I dine earlier (later) tomorrow?	Μπορῶ αὔριο νά φάγω ἐνωρίτερα (ἀργότερα);
	boh-roh' ahv'-re-oh nah fah'-gho en-or-ee'-tair-ah (arr-ghot'-air-ah)
May I have my bill?	Μοῦ δίνετε τόν λογαρι-ασμό;
	mou the'-neh-teh ton logh-are-e-ahz-moh'
Where is my luggage?	Ποῦ εἶναι τά πράγματά μου;
	pou ee'-neh tah pragh-mah-tah'-mou
Would you get me a taxi?	μοῦ φωνάζετε ἕνα ταξί;
	mou for-nahz'-eh-teh en'-nah tax-ee'

Camping and Caravanning

With no fear of rain spoiling your holiday, this is not only the cheapest way of seeing the country but one of the best ways of getting to know the real Greece. There are several organised camping sites, but in addition you are allowed to camp anywhere outside built-up areas. Full details of sites can be had from the Automobile and Touring Club of Greece (ELPA), 6 Amerikis Street, Athens.

Youth Hostels. There are about a dozen hostels run by the Greek Y.H.A., 4 Dragatsaniou Street, Athens, and others that belong to the Federation of Greek Excursionist Clubs (at the same address).

USEFUL WORDS AND PHRASES

boots (οἱ) μπότες, (οἱ) ἀρβύλες (nailed)
  bott'-ess, ar-vee'-less
bridge (ἡ) γέφυρα *yef'-ee-rah*
bucket (ὁ) κουβᾶς *koo-vahss'*
camp (ἡ) κατασκήνωσις *kah-tah-skee'-nos-ees*
camping site (ὁ) χῶρος κατασκηνώσεως
  Hor'-oss kah-tah-ske-noss'-eh-oss
cooking utensils (τά) σκεύη μαγειρικῆς
  skehv'-ee mah-ye-re-kiss'
cork screw (τό) τριμπουσόν *tree-boo-sonn'*
drinking water (τό) πόσιμο νερό *poss'-ee-moh neh-roh'*
east ἀνατολικό *an-ah-tol-e-koh'*
farm (τό) ἀγρόκτημα *ahgh-rock'-te-mah*
farmer (ὁ) γεωργός *yeh-or-ghoss'*
field (ὁ) ἀγρός *ahgh-ross'*
forest (τό) δάσος *thah'-soss*
frying pan (τό) τηγάνι *te-ghan'-ee*
groundsheet (ὁ) μουσαμᾶς κατασκηνώσεως
  moo-sahm-ahs' kah-tah-ske-noss'-eh-oss
hike (ἡ) πεζοπορεία *peh-zo-por-ee'-ah*
hitch hike (τό) ὠτο-στόπ *auto-stop'*
hill (ὁ) λόφος *lof'-oss*
ice (ὁ) πάγος *pah'-ghoss*
lake (ἡ) λίμνη *lim'-nee*
log (ὁ) κορμός δέντρου *kor-moss' then'-troo*
matches (τά) σπίρτα *speer'-tah*
mess tin (τό) ἀγγεῖον φαγητοῦ *ahn-ghee'-on fah-ye-too'*
methylated spirit (τό) οἰνόπνευμα *ee-nop'-nev-mah*
mountain (τό) βουνό *voo-noh'*

35

mountain pass (τό) μονοπάτι *mono-pat'-ee*
north (ό) βορριᾶς *vorr-yas'*
paraffin (τό) πετρέλαιο *pet-rel-eh'-oh*
path (ό) δρομίσκος *throh-mees'-koss*
penknife (ό) σουγιᾶς *soo-yas'*
picnic (ή) ἐκδρομή *eck-throh-mee'*
pole (τό) κονταρόξυλο *kon-dah-rocks'-ee-loh*
river (τό) ποτάμι *pot-am'-ee*
road (ό) δρόμος *throh-moss*
rope (τό) σχοινί *sHe-nee'*
rubbish σκουπίδια *skoo-pee'-the-ah*
refuse bin κάλαθος τῶν ἀχρήστων
         kah'-lah-thoss ton aH-riss'-ton
rucksack γυλιός *yee-lee-oss'*
saucepan κατσαρόλα *kats-ah-roh'-la*
shower (rain) ραγδαία βροχὴ *ragh-they'-ah vroh-Hee'*
sleeping bag σάκκος ὕπνου *sack'-oss eep'-noo*
snow (τό) χιόνι *H'yon'-ee*
south (ό) νότος *not'-oss*
storm (ή) θύελλα *thee'-eh-lah*
stove (ή) θερμάστρα—(ή) σόμπα
         thairr-mahst'-rah sohm'-bah
stream (τό) ποτάμι *pot-am'-ee*
summit (ή) κορυφή *core-ree-fee'*
tent (ή) τέντα—(ή) σκηνή *ten'-tah, ske-nee'*
tent peg (ό) πάσσαλος τέντας *pahs'-sah-lohs ten'-tahs*
thermos (τό) θερμός *thair-mos'*
tin opener (τό) ἀνοιχτήρι κονσερβῶν
         ah-niH-teer'-e kon-sair-von'
torch (ό) φανός τσέπης *fah-noss' tsep'-iss*
valley (ή) κοιλάς *kee-lahs'*

walk (ὁ) περίπατος *pair-ree'-pah-toss*
walk (v.) περπατῶ *pair-pah-torr'*
village (τό) χωριό *Hor-e-oh'*
waterfall (ὁ) καταρράκτης *kat-ah-rack'-tiss*
waterproof (τό) ἀδιάβροχο *ah-the-ahv'-roh-Ho*
weather (bad, good) (ὁ) καιρός (κακός, καλός)
        kay-ah-ross' (*kah-koss'—, kah-loss'—*)
west (ἡ) δύσις *the'-siss*
wind (ὁ) ἄνεμος *an'-eh-moss*
wood (τό) ξύλο *kse'-loh*

May I camp here?   Μπορῶ νά κατασκηνώσω
                        ἐδῶ;
    boh-roh' nah kah-tah-skee-noss'-oh eh-thoh'
Where is the camping site?   Ποῦ εἶναι οἱ κατασκην-
                          ώσεις;
    poo ee'-neh kah-tah-skee-noss'-ees
What is the charge per night? Πόσο στοιχίζει ἡ νυχτιά;
    pos'-soh ste-Hee'-ze ee niH-te-ah'
May we light a fire?   Μποροῦμε νά ἀνάψωμε
                         φωτιά;
    boh-roo'-meh nah ah-nap'-saw-meh foht-yah'
Where can I buy ...?   Ποῦ μπορῶ νά ἀγο-
                         ράσω ...;
    poo boh-roh' nah ah-ghor-ass'-o ...

Motoring

Getting about by car is one of the most enjoyable
ways of sightseeing in Greece. There is far less traffic than

in the U.K. and the main trunk roads are good. But other main roads are often narrow, and many minor roads (even those between towns) are often unmetalled. Signposts are in both Greek and Roman lettering; the latter can nevertheless be confusing due to inconsistent transcription and the fact that place names can end in the nominative or accusative case.

You no longer need an International Driving Permit for Greece. Insurance of foreigners' cars in Greece is not compulsory, but you should nonetheless hold an International (green) Insurance Card. In case of accident, contact: The Motor Insurers Bureau, 6 Dragatsaniou Street, Athens, telephone 235-593 or 221-794.

Drive on the right, overtake on the left. Outside towns, priority at crossroads is given to traffic on the main road. In towns, traffic coming from the right has priority. Do not use your horn in towns except to avoid an accident. International road signs are used throughout the country, and the speed limit in inhabited areas varies according to the nature of the road and other local conditions. While the new highways and other straight, wide roads permit usual high speeds, you must remember that care is essential in built-up areas where traffic is heavy and visibility poor. People are not used to dense, fast-moving traffic, and you should keep below 20 m.p.h. In mountainous areas you should exercise care and not exceed 30 m.p.h., and night driving is best avoided in all country areas.

Road assistance is given free to foreign motorists by the Automobile and Touring Club of Greece (ELPA), whose yellow vehicles operate on most main roads. These vehicles are marked "Assistance Routière A.T.C.G./ ELPA"; they carry spare parts and the drivers can effect repairs and give advice.

Parking is controlled, being permitted without lights on alternate sides of the street according to the time of the month. Police are empowered to tow away cars that are parked and causing an obstruction in main thoroughfares. The narrow streets of most towns makes parking a problem. The central part of Athens is somewhat difficult, but there are special parking places reserved for tourists' cars and indicated by foreign language notices. The largest car park is that in Klafthmonos Square. Also in this part of Athens is a one-way system, with traffic regulated by automatic lights. These are the usual red, amber and green sequence, but elsewhere be on the watch for red and green lights only, hung across the road. The largest garages and service stations are along Syngros Avenue.

USEFUL WORDS AND PHRASES

accelerator (ὁ) ἐπιταχυντής *eh-pe-tah-Hin-tiss'*
back axle (ὁ) ἄξων ὀπισθίων τροχῶν
  ax'-son op-ees-the'-on troch-on'
battery (ἡ) μπαταρία *bah-tah-ree'-ah*
big end (ἡ) κεφαλή στροφάλου *keh-fa-lee' stroh-fah'-loo*
body (τό) ἁμάξωμα, (τό) σασί *ah-max'-oh-mah, sas-si'*
bolt (τό) μπουλόνι *boo-lon'-ee*
bonnet (ἡ) καλύπτρα *kah-lip'-trah*
boot (ὁ) χῶρος ἀποσκευῶν *Hor'-ross ah-pos-keh-von'*
brake, hand- (τό) φρένο, χειρόφρενο
  fren'-oh, He-rof'-fren-oh

39

brake lining (ἡ) φόδρα τοῦ φρένου *foth'-ra too fren'-ou*
breakdown (ἡ) βλάβη *vlah'-vee*
breakdown van (τό) αὐτοκίνητον ἐπισκευῶν
      ahf-toh-kee'-ne-ton eh-pees-keh-von'
bumper (ἡ) σούστα *soos'-tah*
camshaft (ὁ) ἐκκεντροφόρος ἄξων
      ek-ken-droh-for'-oss ax'-son
can (τό) δοχεῖον *thoh-He'-on*
car (τό) αὐτοκίνητο *ahf-toh-kee'-ne-toh*
caravan (τό) καραβάν *kah-rah-van'*
carburettor (τό) καρμπυρατὲρ *kar-bu-rah-terr'*
choke (ὁ) ἐμφράκτης τοῦ καρμπυρατέρ
      em-frak'-tees too kar-bu-rah-terr'
clutch (ὁ) συμπλέκτης, ἀμπραγιάζ
      seem-blek'-tees, ahm-bry-ahz'
distributor (ὁ) διανομεύς *the-ah-no-meffs'*
door (ἡ) πόρτα *por'-tah*
drive (v.) ὁδηγῶ *oh-the-ghoh'*
driver (ὁ) ὁδηγός, σωφέρ *oh-the-ghoss', sof-fair'*
dynamo (τό) δυναμό *the-na-moh'*
engine (ἡ) μηχανή, (τό) μοτέρ *me-Han-ee', moh-terr'*
exhaust (ὁ) σωλήνας ἐξατμίσεως
      so-leen'-ahs ex-at-mees'-ay-oss
fan (ὁ) ἀνεμιστήρ *ahn-ay-mees-teer'*
fan belt (τό) λουρί ἀνεμιστῆρος
      loo-ree' ahn-ay-mees-teer'-oss
funnel (τό) χωνί *Hon-nee'*
garage (τό) γκαράζ *gah-raz'*
gear (ἡ) ταχύτης *tah-Hee'-tiss*
gearbox (τό) κιβώτιον ταχυτήτων
      kee-vot'-ee-on tah-Hee-teet'-on

gear lever (ὁ) μοχλός ταχυτήτων
    moch-loss' tah-Hee-teet'-on
handle (τό) χερούλι *here-oo'-lee*
hood (τό) κάλυμμα, καπό *kah'-lee-mah, kah-poh'*
horn κόρνα *korn'-ah*
hub κέντρον τροχού *ken'-tron troH-oo'*
ignition (ἡ) ἀνάφλεξις *ahn-af'-lex-ees*
ignition key (τό) κλειδί ἀναφλεκτῆρος
    kle-thee' ahn-af-leck-tee'-ross
indicator (ὁ) δείκτης *thik'-tiss*
inner tube (ὁ) ἀεριοθάλαμος, (ἡ) σαμπρέλα
    eye-re-oh-that'ah-moss, sah-brell'-ah
jack (ὁ) γρύλλος *ghre'-loss*
licence (ἡ) ἄδεια *ah'-the-ah*
lights (τά) φῶτα *foh'-tah*
lights (head) μεγάλα φῶτα *megh-ah'-lah foh'-tah*
lights (side) (τά) φῶτα πλευρῶν *foh'-tah plev-vron'*
lights (rear) (τά) φῶτα ὀπίσθια *foh'-tah oh-pees'-the-ah*
lorry (τό) φορτηγό αὐτοκίνητο
    fort-ee-gho' ahf-toh-kee'-ne-toh
lubrication (τό) λάδωμα *lah'-thor-mah*
mechanic (ὁ) μηχανικός *me-han-e-koss'*
mirror (ὁ) καθρέφτης *kah-thref'-tiss*
motorway (ὁ) αὐτοκινητόδρομος
    ahf-toh-ke-ne-toth'-ro-mos
number plate (ἡ) πλάκα ἀριθμοῦ κυκλοφορίας
    plah'-kah ah-rith-mou' kik-lo-fo-ree'-ahs
oil (τό) λάδι *lah'-the*
pedestrian(s) (ὁ) πεζός, (οἱ) πεζοί *peh-zoss', peh-zee'*
petrol (ἡ) βενζίνη *ven-zee'-ne*

petrol pump (τό) Πρατήριον Βενζίνης
prah-teer'-e-on ven-zee'-niss
piston ring (ὁ) δακτύλιος στεγανότητος ἐμβόλου
thak-teel'-e-oss steh-gha-not'-e-toss em-vol'-oo
plug (ὁ) σπινθηρηστήρ *spin-the-ris-teer'*
propeller shaft (ὁ) ἄξων ἕλικος *ax'-son eh'-le-kos*
radiator (τό) ραντιατέρ *rah-de-ah-terr'*
rim (τό) στεφάνι τροχοῦ *stef-ah'-ne troch-oor'*
screw (ἡ) βίδα *vee'-thah*
screwdriver (ὁ) βιδολόγος *ve-thoh-logh'-oss*
shock absorber (ὁ) χαλινωτήρ, (ἡ) σούστα
hal-e-not-eer', soos'-tah
skid (τό) γλύστριμα *ghlee'-strim-ah*
to skid γλυστρώ *ghlee-stroh'*
spanner (τό) βιδωτήρι *ve-tho-teer'-e*
spares (τά) ἀνταλλακτικά *ahn-dah-lahk-te-kah'*
speed (ἡ) ταχύτης *tah-hee'-tiss*
speed limit (τό) ὅριον ταχύτητος
or'-re-oh tah-hee'-tit-oss
speedometer (τό) ταχύμετρον *tach-ee'-met-ron*
spring (τό) ἔλασμα, (ἡ) σούστα *eh'-las-mah, soos'-tah*
starter (ἡ) μανιβέλα *man-e-vell'-ah*
steering wheel (τό) τιμόνι, (τό) βολάν *te-mon'-e vol-an'*
tank (τό) ντεπόζιτο *deh-poz'-'e-toh*
traffic lights (ὁ) σηματοδότης *see-mah-toh-tho'-tiss*
trailer (τό) ρυμουλκό *re-mool-koh'*
transmission (τό) κιβώτιον ταχυτήτων
ke-voht'-e-on tach-e-tee'-ton
two-stroke mixture δίχρονον μίγμα
the'-hron-on meegh'-mah
tyre (τό) λάστιχο *las'-te-ho*

tyre (tubeless) (τό) λάστιχο χωρίς ἀεροθάλαμο
         las'-te-ho hor-rees' eye-re-oh-thal'-ah-mo
valve (ἡ) βαλβίς *val-vees'*
vehicle (τό) ὄχημα *och'-e-mah*
washer (ἡ) ροντέλα *ron-dell'-ah*
wheel (ὁ) τροχός *troch-oss'*
  (rear-, front-) ὀπίσθιος τροχός, ἐμπρόσθιος τροχός
         oh-pees'-the-oss troch-oss', em-pros'-the-
         oss troch-oss'
  (spare-) (ἡ) ρεζέρβα *re-zair'-vah*
window (τό) παράθυρο *pah-rah'-the-roh*
  (rear-) (τό) ὀπίσθιο παράθυρο
       oh-pees'-the-oh pah-rah'-the-roh
windscreen (τό) παρπρίζ *parr-breez'*
windscreen wiper (οτ) καθαριστήρες *kath-ar-iss-teer'-ess*
wing (τό) φτερό *ftair-oh'*

I want some petrol (oil,   Θέλω βενζίνα (λάδι, νερό)
water)
      thel'-oh ven-zee'-na (lath'-ee, neh-roh')
I have run out of petrol   Μοῦ ἔχει τελειώσει ἡ
                    βενζίνη
      moo eH'-ee telly-oss'-e ee ven-zee'-ne
Would you check the oil?   'Εξετάζετε, παρακαλῶ, τήν
                    ποσότητα τοῦ λαδιοῦ;
      eks-eh-tah'-zeh-teh, pah-rah-kah-lo', tin poss-ot'-η-ta
           too lah-the-oo'
Would you check the tyre   'Εξετάζετε, παρακαλω, τήν
pressure?   πίεσι τῶν λαστίχων;
      eks-eh-tah'-zeh-teh, pah-rah-kah-lo', tin pee'-ess-e
           ton lahs-tee'-Hon

Do you do repairs?	Κάνετε ἐπιδιορθώσεις;
	kan'-eh-teh eh-pe-the-orr-thoss'-ees
Can you repair the . . .?	Μπορεῖτε νά μοῦ ἐπισκευάσετε τό . . .
	boh-ree'-teh nah moo eh-pe-skev-ah'-set-teh toh . . .
How long will it take?	Πόσον καιρό θά πάρη;
	poss'-on keh-roh' thah pah'-re
The engine is overheating	Τό μοτέρ ζεσταίνεται πολύ
	toh mo-tair' zes-ten'-eh-teh poll-y'
May I park here?	Μπορῶ νά σταθμεύσω ἐδῶ;
	boh-roh' nah stath-meff'-so eh-thoh'
Where may I park?	Ποῦ μπορῶ νά σταθμεύσω;
	poo boh-roh' nah stath-meff'-so
How far is it to . . .?	Πόση εἶναι ἡ ἀπόστασις ἕως τό . . .
	poss'-ee ee'-neh ee ah-poss'-stass-ees ay'-oss toh . . .
What time does the garage close?	Πότε κλείνει τό γκαράζ;
	poh'-teh klee'-ne toh gah-raz'
My brakes are slipping (binding)	Τά φρένα γλυστροῦν (σφίγγουν)
	tah fren'-ah ghlees-troon' (sfing'-oon)
How far is the next garage?	Πόσο μακρυά βρίσκεται τό ἄλλο γκαράζ;
	poss'-oh mah-kre-ah' vree'-sket-eh toh al'-lo gah-raz'
May I wash my hands?	Μπορῶ νά πλύνω τά χέρια μου;
	boh-roh' nah plee'-noh tah Heh'-re-ah-moo
Where is the toilet, please?	Ποῦ εἶναι τό μέρος, παρακαλῶ;
	poo ee'-neh toh mair'-oss, pah-rah-kah-loh'

May I use your telephone?	Μπορῶ νά χρησιμοποιήσω τό τηλέφωνό σας;
	boh-roh' nah Hree-se-mop-e-ees'-o toh tee-lef-on-oss'-ass
I want a new fanbelt	Θέλω ἕνα νέο λουρί γιά τόν ἀνεμιστῆρα
	thel'-oh en'-nah neh'-oh loor-ee' yah ton ahn-ay-mist-eer'-ah
The clutch is slipping	Τό ἀμπραγιάζ δέν πιάνει, γλιστρᾶ
	toh ahm-bry-ahz' then pe-ahn'-e, ghlees-trah'
Is this the road to . . .?	Αὐτός εἶναι ὁ δρόμος γιά τό . . .
	af-toss' ee'-neh oh throm'-oss yah toh . . .
Would you wipe the wind-screen?	Σφουγγίζετε τό παρμπρίζ;
	sfoong-eez'-eh-teh toh pahr-breez'
Could you clean it right away?	Μπορεῖτε νά τό καθαρίσετε ἀμέσως;
	boh-ree'-teh nah toh kah-thah-rees'-eh-teh ah-mess'-os
May I park without lights?	Μπορῶ νά σταθμεύσω μέ τά φῶτα σβυσμένα;
	bor-roh' nah stath-meff'-so meh tah foh'-tah zvees-men'-ah
I want to hire a car for . . .	Θέλω νά νοικιάσω ἕνα αὐτοκίνητο γιά . . .
	thel'-oh nah nicky-ass'-oh en'-nah ahf-toh-kee'-ne-toh yah . . .
Would you fit a new bulb?	Μπορεῖτε νά βάλετε ἕνα νέο γλόμπο;
	boh-ree'-teh nah vah'-leh-teh en'-nah nay'-oh ghlom'-boh

Would you mend this puncture?	Μπορεῖτε νά μπαλώσετε τό τρυπημένο λάστιχο;
	boh-ree'-teh nah bah-loss'-eh-teh toh tre-pe-men'-oh lahs'-te-Ho
May I borrow . . . ?	Μοῦ δανείζετε . . . ;
	moo than-eez'-eh-teh . . .

Public Transport

BY RAIL

The two state-owned railway systems, SEK (Greek State Railways) and SPAP (Piraeus-Athens-Peloponnese Railways), with new locomotives and modern coaches, maintain regular and comfortable services to the most important regions of the country. The network is otherwise not very extensive. It is best to pay a small surcharge and travel on one of the international express or diesel trains, as others are often slow.

BY AIR

The Civil Aviation Department, in cooperation with the national airline Olympic Airways, has set up an extensive network of air services connecting the large towns, islands and tourist centres. Fares are low, and you may prefer to fly from one place to another rather than waste time going by sea, rail or car; although seeing more of the country by the latter methods, the rugged terrain can make such travelling a slow and tedious affair.

BY COACH, LOCAL TRANSPORT

As the railway network is poor, it is left to the privately owned bus companies to provide links between many provincial areas. This they do very well, and although a lot of inter-urban buses have seen better days they are now quickly being replaced by fast modern vehicles. There is also a large fleet of luxurious "Pullman" coaches, used by travel agencies who run tours to archaeological sites and other places of interest. SEK also operate a few coach services from Athens.

The Athens region has a good local transport network. Buses connect the city centre with the farthest suburb, and these services operate until about midnight. Such seaside places as Phaleron, Glyfada, Voula, Vouliagmeni and Varkiza are all on the urban bus routes, and the fares are cheap.

In addition to the bus services, a few urban routes are served by electric trolleys, and there is an electric railway connecting Piraeus and Kiphissia, via Athens. A considerable number of 4- and 6-seater taxi cabs ply throughout the area, and there are plenty of smaller, less luxurious taxis that are distinguished by the words "Reduced Tariff" painted on the door.

BY BOAT

Not surprisingly in view of the number and importance of the Greek islands, there is an extremely satisfactory network of steamer services, many of which start from Piraeus. There are more than twenty regular domestic ferry-boat services, many of which take cars and thus save one a lot of driving round a peninsula.

USEFUL WORDS AND PHRASES

air hostess (ἡ) ἀεροσυνοδός *ah-air-o-se-no-thoss'*
airline (ἡ) ἀεροπορική γραμμή
        ah-air-o-por-re-kee' ghram-ee'
airport (τό) ἀεροδρόμιο *ah-air-o-thro'-me-on*
alight καταβαίνω *kat-ah-ven'-oh*
berth (*n*.) κοκέττα *cock-yet'-tah*
board ἀναβαίνω, ἐπιβιβάζομαι
        ah-la-ven'-oh, eh-pe-ve-vah'-zo-meh
booking office Ἐκδοτήρια εἰσιτηρίων
           ek-tho-teer'-re-ah ee-se-te-ree'-on
boot (ὁ) χῶρος ἀποσκευῶν *hor'-oss ah-poss-ke-von'*
bus (τό) λεωφορεῖον *lay-off-or-ree'-on*
carriage (τό) βαγόνι *vah-ghon'-ee*
case (ἡ) βαλίτσα *vah-leet'-sah*
cloudy συννεφιασμένος *see-nef-fee-ahz-men'-oss*
coach (τό) λεωφορεῖον *lay-off-or-ree'-on*
compartment (τό) διαμέρισμα *the-ah-meh'-riss-mah*
conductor (ὁ) εἰσπράκτωρ *ees-prak'-tor*
connection (ἡ) σύνδεσις *sin'-the-sis*
corridor (ἡ) διάδρομος *the-ah'-thro-moss*
crew (τό) πλήρωμα *pleer'-oh-mah*
deck κατάστρωμα *cat-ah'-straw-mah*
dining car (τό) ἐστιατόιον *es-te-ah-tor'-re-on*
draught (τό) ρεῦμα *rrev'-mah*
driver (ὁ) ὁδηγός, σωφέρ *oh-the-ghoss', soff-air'*
enquiry office (τό) γραφεῖον πληροφοριῶν
        ghraf-fee'-on plee-roff-or-e-on'
entrance (ἡ) εἴσοδος *ees'-oh-thoss*
exit (ἡ) ἔξοδος *ex'-oh-thoss*

fare (τά) ναῦλα *nahv'-lah*
ferry (*n.*) πορθμεῖον *porth-me'-on*
fog πυκνή ὁμίχλη *pick-ne' oh-me'-Hlee*
front ἐμπρός *em-bross'*
fumes (τά) ἀέρια *eye'-re-ah*
guard (ὁ) φύλακας *fee'-lah-kahs*
jet aircraft (τό) ἀεριωθούμενο
      ah-er-re-oh-thoo'-men-on
land (*v.*) προσγειώνομαι *proz-yeo'-no-meh*
luggage van (τό) βαγόνι ἀποσκευῶν
      vah-ghon'-ee ah-poss-keh-von'
luggage rack (τό) ράφι ἀποσκευῶν
      raf'-ee ah-poss-keh-von'
passenger ἐπιβάτης *eh-pe-vah'-tis*
pilot (ὁ) πιλότος *pee-lot'-oss*
platform (ἡ) πλατφόρμα *plat-for'-mah*
porter (ὁ) ἀχθοφόρος *aH-thoh-for'-os*
quay προκυμαία *pro-ke-me'-ah*
rack (τό) ράφι *raf'-fee*
rear τό ὀπίσω *toh oh-pees'-oh*
roof (ἡ) στέγη *steh'-ghe*
route (ἡ) γραμμή, (τό) δρομολόγιο
      ghram-me', thro-mo-loy'-yo
runway διάδρομος ἀπογειώσεως
      the-ah'-thro-moss ah-poy-yoss'-eh-oss
seat (ἡ) θέσις, (τό) κάθισμα *thess'-sis, kath'-is-mah*
seat belt (ἡ) ζώνη καθίσματος *zon'-ee kath-is'-mah-toss*
seat reservation (ἡ) κράτησις θέσεως
      krah'-te-sis thess'-ay-os
ship πλοῖον *ple'-on*
sleeper (τό) βαγόνι ὕπνου *vah-ghon'-ee ip'-noo*

D   49

sleeping berth (τό) κρεββάτι, (ή) κοκκέτα
    kreh-va'-te, kok-ket'-ah
station (ὁ) σταθμός *stath-moss'*
station master (ὁ) Σταθμάρχης *stath-mar'-Hees*
steward (ὁ) καμαρότος *kah-mah-rot'-oss*
stop (ή) στάσις *stass'-ees*
take-off (ή) ἀπογείωσις *ah-poh-yee'-oh-siss*
terminus (ὁ) τελικός σταθμός, (τό) τέρμα
    telly-koss' stath-moss', tair'-mah
ticket (single) (τό) εἰσιτήριον *issy-teer'-re-on*
  (return) εἰσιτήριον ἐπιστροφῆς
    issy-teer'-re-on eppy-strof-ees'
ticket collector (ὁ) εἰσπράκτωρ *iss-prak'-tor*
timetable (τό) δρομολόγιον *thro-mo-law'-ye-on*
train (τό) τραῖνο, (ή) ἁμαξοστοιχία
    treh'-no, ah-max-ost-e-hee'-ah
waiting room (ή) αἴθουσα ἀναμονῆς
    eth'-oo-sah ah-nam-on-ees'
window (τό) παράθυρον *pah-rah'-the-ro*
wing (τό) φτερό *fteh-roh'*

Where is the (coach)   Ποῦ εἶναι ὁ σταθμὸς (λε-
station?   ωφορείων);
    poo ee'-neh oh stath-moss' (lay-off-or-ee'-on)
I want a single (return)   Θέλω ἕνα εἰσιτήριο (μετ'
ticket to ...   ἐπιστροφῆς) γιά τό ...
    thel'-oh en'-nah issy-teer'-re-oh (met
    eppy-strof-ees') yah toh ...
I have a reserved seat   ἔχω κρατήσει Θέσι
    eh'-Hoh krah-tee'-se thess'-e

Would you find me a seat?   Μπορεῖτε νό μοῦ βρῆτε
                                  θέσι

boh-ree'-teh nah moo vree'-teh thess'-e

I would like a smoking (non   Θέλω διαμέρισμα πού (δέν)
smoking) compartment   ἐπιτρέπεται τό κάπνισμα

thel'-oh the-ah-mair'-is-mah poo (then)
eh-pe-trep'-eh-teh toh kap'-nees-mah

Could I have a window seat?   Θά ἤθελα θέσι κοντά στό
                                  παράθυρο   ;

thah ee'-thel-ah thess'-e kon-dah' stoh pah-rath'-e-ro

This seat is reserved   Αὐτή ἡ θέσις ἔχει κρατηθῆ

af-tee' ee thess'-ees eh'-He krah-te-thee'

That seat is taken   Ἐκείνη ἡ θέσις εἶναι
                                   πιασμένη

eh-kee'-ne ee thess'-ees ee'-neh pe-ahs-men'-e

Could you find me a berth?   Μπορεῖτε νά μοῦ βρῆτε
                                   κρεββάτι;

boh-ree'-teh nah moo vree'-teh kreh-vah'-te

May I open (close) the   Μπορῶ νά ἀνοίξω (κλείσω)
window?   τό παράθυρο;

boh-roh' nah ah-neek'-soh (klee'-soh) toh
pah-rath'-e-ro

How long do we stop here?   Πόσην ὥρα θά σταματή-
                                   σωμε ἐδῶ;

poss'-een or'-rah thah stah-mah-tee'-so-meh eh-thoh'

Please mind my seat   Παρακαλῶ μοῦ φυλάγετε
                                   τήν θέσι μου;

pah-rah-kah-lo' moo fee-lah'-yay-teh teen thess'-e-moo

Which way is the dining car?   Ποῦ βρίσκεται τό ἐστι-
                                   ατόριο;

poo vrees'-ket-eh toh est-e-ah-tor'-e-o

What time is lunch (dinner)? Τί ὥρα εἶναι τό γεῦμα
(δεῖπνο);
tee or'-rah ee'-neh toh yev'-mah (theep'-noh)

What time do you leave Τί ὥρα φεύγετε (φθάνετε);
(arrive)?
tee or'-rah fev'-yeh-teh (fthan'-eh-teh)

Where is the inspector? Ποῦ εἶναι ὁ ἐπιθεωρητής;
poo ee'-neh oh eppy-thay-orry-teese'

I want to get off at ... Θέλω νά βγῶ στό ...
thel'-oh nah ev'-gho stoh ...

Will you tell me when we Μοῦ λέτε πότε φθάνομε;
arrive? *moo leh'-teh poh'-teh fthan'-o-meh*

Do you pass ...? Περνᾶτε ἀπό τό ...
pair-nah'-teh ah-poh' toh ...

Do you go near ...? Πηγαίνετε κοντά στό ...;
pee-yen'-eh-teh kon-dah' stoh ...

Will you put this on the roof Βάζετε παρακαλῶ αὐτό
(in the boot)? στην σκέπη; (στόν χῶρο
τῶν ἀποσκευῶν);
*vah'-zeh-teh pah-rah-kah-lo' af'-toh stin skep'-e
(ston Hor'-o ton ah-poss-keh-von')*

There is a draught Κάνει ρεῦμα
kah'-ne rrev'-mah

Would you please open Σᾶς παρακαλῶ ἀνοίξετε
(close) the window (κλείσετε) τό παράθυρο
*sahs pah-rah kah-lo' ah-neeks'-et-eh (klees'-et-eh)
toh pah-rath'-e-ro*

May I put this on the rack? Μπορῶ νά βάλω αὐτό στό
ράφι;
boh-roh' nah vah'-loh af-toh' stoh rahf'-ee

Do you return here?	Ἐπιστρέφετε ἀπ' ἐδῶ;
	eh-pe-stref'-eh-teh up eh-thoh'
Do you start from here?	Ἀναχωρεῖτε ἀπ' ἐδῶ;
	ah-nah-Hor-ee'-teh up eh-thoh'
Porter, can you take this luggage to the left-luggage office?	Παρακαλῶ, παίρνετε αὐτή τνὴ βαλίτσα στὴν ἀποθήκη ἀποσκευῶν;
	pah-rah-kah-lo', pair'-neh-teh af-tee' tin vah-leed'-sa stin ah-poh-thee'-ke ah-pos-kev-on'
I shall collect it at/on ...	Θά τὴν παραλάβω στάς/τὴν
	thah tin pah-rah-la'-voh stass/tin
Would you get me a taxi to ...	Θέλω ταξί νά μέ πάγη στό ...
	thel'-oh tax-ee' nah meh pah'-ghe stoh ...
Where is the booking office?	Ποῦ εἶναι τά ἐκδοτήρια εἰσιτηρίων;
	poo ee'-neh ta eck-tho-tee'-re-ah ees-e-te-ree'-on
Where is the enquiry office?	Ποῦ εἶναι τό Γραφεῖον Πληροφοριῶν;
	poo ee'-neh toh ghraff-ee'-on plee-roh-for-e-on'
What time does the train leave for ...?	Τί ὥρα φεύγει τό τραῖνο γιά ...;
	tee or'-rah fev'-ye toh treh'-no yah ...
Which platform, please?	Ποιά πλατφόρμα, παρα-καλῶ;
	pe-ah' plat-for'-mah, pah-rah-kah-lo'
Is this the right train for ...?	Αὐτό εἶναι τό τραῖνο γιά ...;
	af-toh' ee'-neh toh treh'-no yah ...
Does it go direct?	Πηγαίνει κατ' εὐθεῖαν;
	pe-yen'-e kat ef-thee'-ahn

53

change?	Πρέπει νά ἀλλάξω;
	prep'-e nah ah-lahx'-o
where do I change?	Ποῦ πρέπει νά ἀλλάξω;
	poo prep'-e nah ah-lahx'-o
What time is the last train for . . .?	Πότε εἶναι τό τελευταῖο τραῖνο γιά . . .;
	poh'-teh ee'-neh toh teh-left-ay'-o treh'-no yah . . .
Where is the nearest hotel?	Ποῦ εἶναι τό πλησιέστερο ξενοδοχεῖο;
	póo ee'-neh toh plee-se-est'-air-o ksay-no-tho-He'-o
When can I get a plane for . . .?	Πότε ὑπάρχει ἀεροπλάνο γιά . . .;
	poh'-teh e-parr'-He ah-air-o-plan'-o yah . . .
What time does it leave (arrive)?	Τί ὥρα ἀναχωρεῖ (φθάνει);
	tee or'-rah ahn-ah Hor-ee' (fthah'-nee)
Where does it touch down?	Ποῦ σταματᾶ;
	poo stah-mah-tah'
Will you fasten (unfasten) my safety belt?	Μοῦ δένετε (λύνετε) τήν ζώνην ἀσφαλείας;
	moo then'-eh-teh (leen'-eh-teh) tin zon'-e ass-fahl-ee'-ahs
Have you a map of the route?	Ἔχετε κανένα χάρτην τοῦ ταξειδίου;
	eh'-Heh-teh kah-nen'-ah Har'-teen too tax-e-thee'-oo
Will you adjust my seat?	Μοῦ διορθώνετε τό κάθισμά μου;
	moo thee-or-thon'-eh-teh toh kah'-thees-ma'-moo
What is the weather report?	Τί εἶναι τά προγνωστικά τοῦ καιροῦ;
	tee ee'-neh tah progh-nos-te-kah' too keh-roo'

May I have some cigarettes (brandy)?	Θέλω σιγαρέττα (κονιάκ)

thel'-oh see-gar-ett'-a (kon-yak')

Are we on time?	Εἴμαστε στήν ὧρα;

ee-mahs'-teh stin or'-ah

Would you adjust the air conditioner?	Κανονίζετε, παρακαλῶ, τό μηχάνημα κλιματισμοῦ;

kah-no-neez'-eh-teh, pah-rah-kah-lo', toh me-han'-e-mah kle-mah-tees-moo'

It is very warm	Κάνει μεγάλη ζέστη

kah'-ne meh-ghal'-e zest'-e

I do not feel well	Δέν αἰσθάνομαι καλά

then ess-thahn'-o-meh kah-lah'

Food and Wine

The best place to eat is where the Greeks eat—in a taverna. You are expected to go into the kitchen and choose what you want from an enormous selection, and you can get an excellent meal for less than £1 although it is as well to beware of the occasional tourist trap. There are countless tavernas in the Plaka quarter of Athens and you will find many more throughout Greece and the islands. In fact it is never hard to find somewhere to eat, and even in the high-class restaurants, where settings are lavish, prices tend to be much lower than in the United Kingdom.

Here are a few suggestions to help you cope with the varied menu:

First course: *Dolmades* are vine leaves stuffed with spicy minced meat and (sometimes) rice, steamed, and covered with a tangy egg and lemon sauce. In one variation, cabbage leaves replace the vine leaves. *Tzatziki* is cucumber with garlic and yoghourt.

Soup: *Mayritsa* is made with thin slices of lamb, lettuce, egg, fennel, and seasoned with the ever-present lemon juice.

Fish: The Greeks excel at cooking fish. Try *Garithes* (shrimps) with tomatoes, oven baked and served with fresh cheese and fine herbs. If you don't like shrimps, try *Taramosalata*; this is a salad of fish roes and mashed potato, with olive oil and lemon seasoning.

Main course: You are very likely to sample the ever-popular *Moussaka*—baked aubergine (eggplant), minced meat and vegetables cooked as a sort of shepherd's pie, often topped with grated cheese. Then there is *Pastichio*, which is mince and spaghetti, baked with vegetables and completed by a bechamel sauce.

To finish, ask for *Baklava*—a honey-cake made with nuts and cinnamon (and extremely sticky)—or fresh fruit. Finally, a strong Greek coffee.

Among the many other delectable Greek dishes which you should try are *Kakavia*, the bouillabaisse of Greece, and *Barbounia* (red mullet). There are giant prawns, and lobster, and fried *kalamares* (squids). If you like garlic, *Skorthalia* is a strong garlic sauce often served with salt cod. You will find plenty of aubergines, courgettes and tomatoes. Lamb is plentiful and comes served in a variety of ways—and can sometimes be disappointing. It is cooked as a kebab, served with paté, fricasséed, roast and boiled. Try also *Loukoumathes*, a delicious fritter made with honey and cinnamon, and among the ices "fruit sorbet" is very tasty.

Despite old rumours, there is no right or wrong time to eat certain meats in Greece, but you might consider the following suggestions: From Easter to October veal is recommended; during the winter suckling pork is the popular dish; from Christmas to Easter try the succulent baby lamb which is then at its best. Greek seafood is simply delicious all the year round.

Drinks

The popular Greek aperitif is *Ouzo*; this is aniseed flavoured and made from crushed grape stems. It is often sipped with snacks known as *Mezes*. Try it with water and ice (2 parts Ouzo to 1 part water). The wine of the country is *Retzina*, which is a resinated wine and an acquired taste. Less resinated is a rosé variety called *Kokkineli*, and there are also bottled red, white and rosé wines, dry, demi-sec and sweet, from almost every region of Greece. Greek beer is very refreshing as it is always served ice-cold.

Most cafes as a rule offer only Greek (or Turkish) coffee, although the more modern establishments in the centre of Athens also serve "espresso". Also provided is a spoonful of jam. There are some 36 ways of making coffee in Greece. *Varigliko* is thick and sweet, *Glikivrasto* is light and sweet, and *Sketo* is without sugar. If you want a normal cup of light, slightly sweetened coffee, you must ask for a *Metrio*. Anything else could prove disastrous if you are fussy about your coffee.

Finally, remember that lunch is served from 1 pm to 3 pm and dinner from 8 pm until the early hours of the morning. If you want to call the waiter, clap your hands and say "garsoni, parakalo".

USEFUL WORDS FOR THE RESTAURANT AND CAFE

GENERAL

bar (τό) μπάρ *bar*
bill (ὁ) λογαριασμός *logh-ah-re-as-moss'*
bottle (τό) μπουκάλι *boo-kah'-lee*
cup (τό) φλυτζάνι *flit-zahn'-ee*
drink (*v.*) πίνω, (*n.*) (τό) ποτό *pee'-noh, poh-toh'*
egg cup (ἡ) αὐγοθήκη *ahv-ghoth-ee'-kee*
fork (τό) πηρούνι *pe-roo'-nee*
glass (τό) ποτήρι *pot-eer'-ee*
knife (τό) μαχαίρι *mach-hair'-ee*
menu (ὁ) κατάλογος φαγητῶν *kat-ah'-logh-oss fah-ye-ton'*
napkin (ἡ) πετσέτα *pets-et'-ah*
plate (τό) πιάτο *pee-at'-oh*
spoon (τό) κουτάλι *koo-tahl'-ye*
table (τό) τραπέζι *trah-pez'-ee*
tip (τό) φιλοδώρημα, πούρ μπουάρ
     feel-oh-thor'-ee-mah, poohr-bwahr'
waiter (ὁ) σερβιτόρος, (τό) γκαρσόνι
     ser-ve-tor'-ross, gar-sonn'-ee
waitress (ἡ) σερβιτόρα *ser-ve-tor'-rah*
wine list (ὁ) κατάλογος κρασιῶν
     kat-ah'-logh-oss krass-e-on'

FOOD

apple (τό) μῆλο *mee'-loh*
banana (ἡ) μπανάνα *banana*

beans (τά) φασόλια *fah-so'-lee-ah*
beef (τό) βωδινό *voh-the-noh'*
biscuit (τό) μπισκότο *bis-kott'-oh*
bread (τό) ψωμί *pso-mee'*
butter (τό) βούτυρο *voo'-teer-oh*
cabbage (τό) λάχανο *lach'-ah-noh*
cake (τό) κέϊκ *kay'-ik*
carrots (τά) καρότα *kah-rot'-ah*
cauliflower (τό) κουνουπίδι *koo-noo-pee'-thee*
cheese (τό) τυρί *teer-ee'*
chops (οί) κοτολέτες, (οί) μπριζόλες
    kot-o-let'-ess, briz-oh'-less
cream (ή) κρέμα, άφρόγαλα *cray'-mah, ah-frogh'-ah-lah*
egg (τό) αὐγό *ahv-ghoh'*
fish (τό) ψάρι *psah'-ree*
fruit (τά) φροῦτα *froo'-tah*
grapes (τά) σταφύλια *stah-feel'-yah*
ham (τό) ζαμπόν *zahm-bon'*
ice-cream (τό) παγωτό *pagh-ot-oh'*
jam (ή) μαρμελάδα, (τό) γλυκό
    mar-meh-lah'-thah, ghle-koh'
lamb (τό) ἀρνί, ἀρνάκι *ar-nee', ar-nak'-ee*
lemon (τό) λεμόνι *leh-mo'-nee*
lobster (ό) ἀστακός *ast-ah-koss'*
marmalade (ή) μαρμελάδα *mar-meh-lah'-thah*
melon (τό) πεπόνι *peh-pon'-ee*
mushrooms (τά) μανητάρια *mahn-e-tar'-re-ah*
mussels (τά) μύδια *mee'-theiah*
mustard (ή) μουστάρδα *moos-tar'-thah*
oil (τό) λάδι *lath'-ee*
onions (τά) κρεμμύδια *kreh-mee'-the-ah*

orange (τό) πορτοκάλλι *por-toh-kah'-lee*
oysters (τό) στρείδι *stree'-the*
parsley (ὁ) μαϊντανός *my-in-da-noss'*
peach (τό) ροδάκινο *roth-ak'-e-noh*
pear (τό) ἀχλάδι *ach-lath'-ee*
peas (τά) μπιζέλια, (ὁ) ἀρακᾶς *be-zell'-ya, ah-rah-kass'*
pepper (τό) πιπέρι *pee-pair'-ee*
pork (τό) χοιρινό *heer-in-oh'*
potatoes (οἱ) πατάτες *pah-tah'-tess*
poultry (τά) πουλερικά *poo-leh-re-kah'*
rice (τό) ρύζι *ree'-zee*
roll (τό) ψωμάκι *psoh-mah'-ke*
salad (ἡ) σαλάτα *sah-lah'-tah*
salt (τό) ἁλάτι *ah-lah'-te*
sauce (ἡ) σάλτσα *sahl'-tsah*
scampi μεγάλες γαρίδες *meh-ghal'-ess ghah-ree'-thess*
shrimps (οἱ) γαρίδες *ghah-ree'-thess*
soup (ἡ) σούπα *soo'-pah*
sugar (ἡ) ζάχαρη *zach'-ah-ree*
toast (ἡ) φρυγανιά *frigh-ahn-yah'*
tomatoes (οἱ) ντομάτες *doh-mah'-tess*
vanilla (ἡ) βανίλλια *vah-neel'-yah*
veal (τό) μοσχάρι, (τό) βιδέλο
    mos-Hah'-ree, vee-thel'-lo
vegetables (τά) χορταρικά *hor-tah-re-kah'*
  (greens) (τά) λαχανικά *lach-ahn-ee-kah'*
vinegar (τό) ξύδι *ksee'-the*

DRINKS

aperitif (τό) ὀρεκτικό *or-ek-te-koh'*
beer (ἡ) μπύρα *beer'-ah*

brandy (τό) κονιάκ *kon-yak'*
chocolate (ή) σοκολάτα *sok-oh-lah'-tah*
coffee (ό) καφφές *kaf-fess'*
gin (τό) τζίν *gin*
ice (ό) πάγος *pagh'-oss*
lemonade (ή) λεμονάδα *lem-on-ah'-thah*
liqueur (τό) λικέρ *le-kair'*
milk (τό) γάλα *ghah'-lah*
mineral water (ή) γαζόζα *ghah-zo'-zah*
orangeade (ή) πορτοκαλλάδα *por-to-kah-lah'-thah*
port (τό) πόρτ *port*
rum (τό) ροῦμι *roo'-me*
soda water (ή) σόδα *soh'-thah*
tea (τό) τσάϊ *tsah'-ee*
water (τό) νερό *neh-roh'*
whisky (τό) γουῖσκι *wisky*
wine (τό) κρασί *krah-see'*

USEFUL PHRASES FOR THE RESTAURANT

May I have a table?   Μπορῶ νά ἔχω ἕνα τραπέζι;
    boh-roh' nah eh'-Ho en'-nah trah-pez'-e
May we have a snack?   Μποροῦμε νά ἔχωμε
                              μερικούς μεζέδες;
    boh-roo'-meh nah eh'-Ho-meh meh-re-koos'
            meh-zeh'-thess
We are in a hurry   βιαζόμεθα (βιαζόμαστε)
    vee-ah-zom'-eh-thah (vee-ah-zom'-ast-eh)
May I have the menu?   Μπορῶ νά ἔχω τόν κατά-
                              λογο φαγητῶν;
    boh-roh' nah eh'-Ho ton kah-tah'-logh-o fah-ye-ton'

61

Have you any English dishes? Έχετε ἀγγλικά φαγητά;

eh'-Heh-teh ahn-glee-kah' fah-e-tah'

I do not like highly seasoned food Δέν μ'ἀρέσουν τά βαρειά φαγητά

then mah-ress'-oon tah var-ya' fah-ye-tah'

I like it well done Τό θέλω καλοψημένο

toh thel'-oh kah-lops-e-men'-oh

Medium, under-done μέτριο, ὄχι πολυψημένο

met'-re-o, oH'-he pol-e-ips-e-men'-o

May I have some bread? Λίγο ψωμί παρακαλῶ

lee'-ghoh psom-ee' pah-rah-kah-lo'

I will have the set lunch (dinner) Θέλω τό καθωρισμένο γεῦμα (δεῖπνο)

thel'-oh toh kah-thor-eez-men'-o yev'-ma (theep'-noh)

A little more, please 'Ακόμα ὀλίγο, παρακαλῶ

ah-kom'-mah oh-lee'-ghoh, pah-rah-kah-lo'

That is enough ἀρκεῖ

ar-kee'

May I have the wine list? Μοῦ δίνετε τόν κατάλογο κρασιῶν;

moo thee'-net-eh ton kah-tah'-logh-o krass-e-on'

May I have a (½) flask of local red (white) wine? Μοῦ φέρνετε παρακαλῶ (μισό) μπουκάλι κόκκινο (ἄσπρο) ντόπιο κρασί;

moo fair'-net-eh pah-rah-kah-lo' (me-soh') boo-kah'-le kok'-ke-noh (ahs'-pro) dop'-pe-oh krass-ee'

I like dry (sweet) wine Θέλω μπροῦσκο (γλυκό) κρασί

thel'-oh broos'-koh (ghlee-koh') krass-ee'

May I have some water? Μπορῶ νά ἔχω λίγο νερό;
 boh-roh' na eh'-Ho lee'-ghoh neh-roh'

May I have some coffee? Μπορῶ νά ἔχω λίγο καφφέ;
 boh-roh' na eh'-Ho lee'-ghoh kaf-feh'

I do not like fat δέν μοῦ ἀρέσει τό παχύ
 then moo ah-ress'-e toh paH-ee'

What do you recommend? Τί συνιστᾶτε;
 tee sin-e-stat'-eh

Would you bring me an Μοῦ φέρνετε ἕνα σταχτο-
ash-tray? δοχεῖο παρακαλῶ;
 moo fair'-net-eh en'-nah staH-toh-tho-hee'-oh,
 pah-rah-kah-lo'

I will come back θά ἐπιστρέψω
 thah epp-y-strep'-soh

May I reserve a table Μπορεῖτε νά μοῦ κρα-
for ...? τήσετε ἕνα τραπέζι γιά ...
 boh-ree'-teh na moo kra-tee'-set-eh en'-nah
 tra-pez'-ee yah ...

May I have the bill? Μοῦ δίνετε τόν λογαρι-
 ασμό, παρακαλῶ;
 moo thee'-net-eh ton logh-ah-re-as-moh',
 pah-rah-kah-lo'

The meal was excellent τό φαγητό ἦταν ὑπέροχο
 (θαυμάσιο)
 toh fah-ye-toh' ee'-tan ee-pair'-o-Ho (thahv-mass'-e-o)

Shopping

In Athens and the principal towns shopping is a real
adventure as the articles for sale, representative of the
popular Greek arts and crafts, are drawn from all over

the country, and very reasonably priced. Shopping hours are from 8 am to 1.30 pm and from 5 pm to 8 pm from May to October. Food shops, barbers and hairdressers are closed on Wednesday afternoons and all other shops on Saturday afternoons. Cafes and confectioners are also open on Sundays and there are always restaurants open on Sundays. In the Plaka district of Athens you will find colourful little market stalls jostled together where you can buy slippers made of red and black leather with poms-poms on them (*Tsarouchia*), belts from Palikare called *Selachia*, beautifully embroidered children's clothes, handbags, bracelets and earrings, and copper coffee mills. The merchants speak English, French and German and are quite prepared to bargain over the price of their wares unless the goods carry a firm price ticket, in which case they are usually adamant.

There are Graeco-Roman antiquities to buy, but first ascertain from the merchant that you can export them. If it is an imitation he will tell you quite truthfully and fix his price accordingly. You will find old coins and pottery, dug up from nearby fields; icons, both crude and exquisitely fashioned; metal crosses, Turkish pistols and swords, rugs and old utensils in copper and brass. You will discover the most surprising bric-a-brac. Saints' medals, medals from a long-lost Balkan nobility, silverware, china, hookahs and mats of traditional design.

Pandrossou Street at Monastiraki in Athens is the place for antiques, handwoven skirts, lace, and dolls dressed in regional costume. In nearby Ifestou Street, named after Ifestos the god of fire, the smiths still hammer away in their roadside forges. And don't forget the honey and the raisins, the wines and the pistachio nuts.

The best shops in Athens are to be found in Jan Smuts (Voucourestiou) and Amerikis Streets, in the upper part of Stadiou and El. Venizelou Streets, around Syntagma Square and in Hermou Street (which is noted for women's wear). On Saturdays and Sunday mornings you can rummage among the treasures of the flea-market —the "Demopratirion"—at Monastiraki where sometimes you may discover furniture, pottery and other objects of excellent workmanship at ridiculously low prices.

A tradition handed down from ancient times has resulted in regional specialization in certain handicraft products. In Arachova, for example, they specialize in colourfully patterned hand-woven woollen blankets, large bags known as *Tagaria* and other such articles. The Ioannina region produces silverware and ornaments of a very original style that are known as *Yanniotika*. Rhodes also produces gold and silver ornaments, of a different pattern, called *Rhoditika*. Mykonos is famous for its weaving and embroidery, Vytina and Metsova for their wood carvings, Kalamata for its silks, and Kastoria for its world-renowned fur-trimming trade.

Of particular interest to foreign visitors are woollen suitings and cotton goods, which are available in a large variety of patterns and colours. The Greek textile industry is backed by a long-standing tradition, and Greek textiles are the equal of any produced abroad. The shoemaking craft is also highly developed. Because labour charges in Greece are on the whole lower than elsewhere, locally

manufactured articles of good quality are generally
cheaper than those you would buy at home, while imported items are naturally much more expensive.

USEFUL WORDS AND PHRASES

GENERAL

ball point πέννα μέ σφαιρίδιον
    pen'-nah mes-fair-ee'-the-on
belt (ή) ζώνη *zonn'-e*
blouse (ή) μπλούζα *bloo'-zah*
book (τό) βιβλίο *viv-lee'-oh*
bracelet (τό) βραχιόλι *vrach-yo'-lee*
braces (οί) τιράντες *te-ran'-dess*
brassiere (τό) σουτιέν, (ό) στηθόδεσμος
    soo-te-en', stee-tho'-thes-moss
brooch (ή) καρφίτσα τοῦ λαιμοῦ
    kar-feets'-ah tuh-lay-muh'
button (τό) κουμπί *koom-bee'*
cap (ή) σκούφια *skoo'-fe-ah*
cigars (τά) ποῦρα *poohr'-ah*
cigarettes (τά) σιγαρέττα, τσιγάρα
    sig-ah-ret'-tah, se-gah' ah
coat (τό) σακάκι *sa-kak'-e*
dictionary (τό) λεξικό *lex-e-koh'*
doll (ή) κούκλα *kook'-lah*
dress (τό) φόρεμα *for'-e-mah*
ear rings (τά) σκουλαρίκια *skoo-lah-reek'-yah*
elastic (τό) λάστιχο *las'-te-Hoh*
envelope (ό) φάκελλος *fah'-keh-loss*
gloves (τά) γάντια *ghan'-te-ah*

gramophone record δίσκος γραμμοφώνου
this'-koss ghrah-moh-fon'-oo
guide book (ὁ) ὁδηγός *oth-e-ghoss'*
handbag (ἡ) τσάντα *tsan'-dah*
handkerchiefs (τά) μαντήλια *man-dee'-le-ah*
hat (τό) καπέλλο *ka-pell'-o*
ink (τό) μελάνι *meh-lahn'-e*
jacket (ἡ) ζακέττα *zak-et'-ah*
jumper (τό) πουλόβερ *pool-o'-ver*
lace (ἡ) δαντέλα *than-tel'-lah*
lighter (ὁ) ἀναπτήρας *ahn-ahp-teer'-ahs*
lighter flint (τό) τσακμάκι *tsahk-mahk'-ee*
lighter fuel βενζίνη ἀναπτῆρος
ven-zee'-nee ahn-ahp-teer'-oss
lighter gas ἀέριον ἀναπτῆρος
eye-air'-e-on ahn-ahp-teer'-oss
map (ὁ) χάρτης *Har'-tees*
matches (τά) σπίρτα *speer'-tah*
necklace (τό) κολιέ, (τό) περιδέραιον
kol-yeh', perry-there'-re-on
needle (ἡ) βελόνη *veh-lon'-ee*
newspaper (ἡ) ἐφημερίδα *effy-meh-ree'-thah*
nightdress (τό) νυκτικό *nik-te-koh'*
nylons (τό) νάϋλον *ny'-lon*
pants (τά) ἐσώβρακα *es-ov'-rah-kah*
pen (ἡ) πέννα *pen'-nah*
pencil (τό) μολύβι *moh-lee'-vee*
petticoat (τό) κομπιναιζόν, (τό) μισοφόρι
kom-be-nay-zon', me-sof-or'-e
pipe (ἡ) πίπα *pee'-pah*
pin (ἡ) καρφίτσα *kar-feets'-ah*

purse (τό) Πορτοφόλι, (τό) πουγγί
  por-toh-foh'-lee, poon-ge'
pyjamas (ή) πυτζάμα *peet-za'-mah*
ring (τό) δακτυλίδι *thak-te-lee'-the*
sandals (τά) σανδάλια *san-tha'-le-ah*
scarf (τό) κασκόλ *kas-koll'*
scissors (τό) ψαλίδι *psal-ee'-the*
shawl (τό) σάλι *sah'-lee*
shirt (τό) πουκάμισο *poo-kah'-me-soh*
shoes (τά) παπούτσια *pah-poot'-se-ah*
shoe polish μπογιά (*or* βερνίκι) παπουτσιῶν
  bugh-yah' (*vair-neek'-ee*) *pah-poot-see-on'*
shoe laces κορδόνια τῶν παπουτσιῶν
  kor-thon'-yah pap-oot-see-on'
silk μετάξι, (τό) μεταξωτό *meh-tax'-ee, meh-tax-o-toh'*
skirt (ή) φούστα *foo'-stah*
slip (τό) μισοφόρι *me-soh-for'-e*
slippers (οί) παντόφλες *pahn-dof'-less*
soap (τό) σαπούνι *sah-poo'-nee*
socks (οί) κάλτσες, (τά) σοσόνια *kalt'-sess, sos-on'-yah*
spectacles (τά) γυαλιά *yal-yah'*
stockings (οί) νάϋλον κάλτσες *ny'-lon kalt'-sess*
strap (τό) λουρί *loor-ee'*
string (ό) σπάγγος *spahn'-goss*
suit (man's) (τό) κουστούμι *kos-too'-me*
(woman's) (τό) ταγιέρ *ty-yair'*
suitcase (ή) βαλίτσα *vah-leets'-ah*
thread (ή) κλωστή *kloss-tee'*
tie (ή) γραβάτα *ghrah-vah'-tah*
tobacco-pouch (ή) καπνοσακκούλα *kap-nos-ack-ool'-ah*
toy (τό) παιχνίδι *peH-nee'-the*

trousers (τά) παντελόνια *pahn-del-on'-yah*
umbrella (ή) όμπρέλλα *om-brell'-ah*
undies (τά) έσώρρουχα *ess-or'-roo Hah*
wallet (τό) πορτοφόλι, χαρτοφυλάκιον
    por toh-fohl'-ee, Har-toh-feel-yak'-e-on
watch (τό) ρολόγι *roh-loy'-e*
wool (τό) μαλλί *mah-lee'*
writing paper χαρτί άλληλογραφίας
    Har-tee' ahl-ee-logh-rah-fee'-ahs

I want to buy ...   θέλω νά άγοράσω ...
    thel'-oh na ah-ghor-ass'-o ...
Will you show me some ...   μοΰ δείχνετε μερικά
    moo theeH'-net-eh mair-ee-ka' ...
Have you anything cheaper   έχετε τίποτα πιό φθηνό
(dearer)?   (άκριβό);
    eh'-Het-eh tee'-pot-a p'yoh fthee-noh' (ah-kree-voh')
Have you anything smaller   έχετε τίποτε πιό μικρό
(bigger)?   (μεγάλο);
    eh'-Het-eh tee'-pot-eh p'yoh mee-kroh' (megh-al'-oh)
Do you have it in other   Τό έχετε σέ άλλα χρώματα;
colours?
    toh eh'-Het-eh seh ah'-lah Hro'-ma-ta
Can you match this colour?   Μπορεΐτε νά ταιριάσετε
                             αύτό τό χρώμα;
    boh-ree'-teh na tair-yahs'-et-eh af-toh' toh Hro'-ma
That's what I want   Αύτό εΐναι έκεΐνο πού θέλω
    af-toh' ee'-neh ek-kee'-noh poo thel'-o
Will you deliver it (them)?   Μπορεΐτε νά μοΰ τό (τά)
                            στείλετε;
    boh-ree'-teh na moo toh (tah) stee'-let-eh

I will collect it later	Θά ἔλθω ἀργότερα νά τό παραλάβω
	thah el'-tho ar-ghot'-air-ah na toh pah-rah-lah'-voh
It is not suitable	Δέν εἶναι κατάλληλο
	then ee'-neh kah-tah'-lee-loh
Could you put it (them) in a box for me?	Μοῦ τό (τά) βάζετε σέ ἔνα κουτί, παρακαλῶ;
	moo toh (tah) vah'-zet-eh seh en'-nah koo-tee', pah-rah-kah-lo'
May I have a receipt?	Μοῦ δίδετε παρακαλῶ ἀπόδειξιν;
	moo thee'-net-eh pah-rah-kah-lo' ah-poh'-theek-sin
Can you let me have it by ...?	Θά μπορούσατε νά μοῦ τό παραδώσετε ὄχι ἀργότερα ἀπό ...
	thah boh-roo'-sah-teh na moo toh pah-rah-thoss'-et-eh oh'-He ar-ghot'-air-ah ah-poh'
May I try it (them)?	Μπορῶ νά τό (τά) προβάρω;
	boh-roh' na toh (tah) prov-are'-oh
Can you repair this?	Μπορεῖτε νά μοῦ ἐπιδιcρθώσετε(μαντάρετε)αὐτό;
	boh-ree'-teh na moo eppy-thee-orr-thoss'-eh-teh (mahn-dar'-et-eh) af'-toh
Can you have it invisibly mended?	Μπορεῖτε νά τό ἐπιδιορθώσετε χωρίς νά φαίνεται;
	boh-ree'-teh nah toh eppy-thee-orr-thoss'-eh-teh Hor-ees - ra fen'-eh-teh
How long will it take?	Πόσον καιρό θά πάρη;
	poss'-on keh-roh' :ha par'-ee

THE CHEMIST

aspirin (ἡ) ἀσπιρίνη *ahs-peer-reen'-e*
bath salts ἁλάτι λουτροῦ *ah-la'-te, loo-troo'*
cotton wool (τό) βαμβάκι *vahm-va'-ke*
cough mixture σιρόπι γιά τόν βήχα
        seer-op'-e ya tonn vee'-Ha
gargle (ἡ) γαργάρα *gar-ghah'-rah*
laxative (τό) καθαρκτικόν, καθάρσιον
        kath-ark-te-kon', kah-thars'-e-on
lipstick (τό) κραγιόν, κοκκινάδι *kry-yon', kok-e-nath'-e*
medicine (τό) φάρμακον *far'-ma-kon*
nail file (ἡ) λίμα τῶν νυχιῶν *lee'-ma ton-ee-He-on'*
ointment (ἡ) ἀλοιφή *al-e-fee'*
plaster (τό) τσιρότο *tseer-ot'-o*
powder (face) (ἡ) πούδρα *pooth'-ra*
razor blades (οἱ) λεπίδες, (τά) ξυραφάκια
        lep-ee'-thess, kse-ra-fak'-e-a
sanitary towels πετσέτες περιόδου
        pet-set'-ess peh-re-oh'-thoo
scissors (τό) ψαλίδι *psa-lee'-the*
soap (τό) σαπούνι *sa-poon'-e*
sun glasses (τά) γυαλιά ἡλίου *yal-ya' il-ee'-oo*
sun-tan lotion λοσιόν γιά ἡλιόκαυμα
        lo-se-on' ya il-e-ok'-av-ma
talcum powder πούδρα τάλκ *pooth'-ra talc*
throat pastilles παστίλιες γιά τόν πονόλαιμο
        pas-teel'-yess ya tonn pon-ol'-em-o
toilet paper χαρτί τουαλέττας *harr-tee' too-a-let'-ass*
tooth brush βούρτσα δοντιῶν *voort'-sa thon-de-on'*
tooth paste (ἡ) ὀδοντόπαστα *o-thon-dop'-as-ta*

71

Can you make up this prescription?	Μπορεῖτε νά μοῦ ἐτοιμάσετε αὐτή τήν συνταγή;
	boh-ree'-teh na moo etty-ma'-set-eh af-tee' tin sin-da-yee'
Could you let me have something for . . .?	Ἔχετε τίποτε γιά . . .;
	eh-Het-eh tee'-pot-eh yah . . .
Upset stomach	Στομαχική διατάραξι
	stom-aH-e-kee' the-ah-tar'-ax-e
Headache. Indigestion	Πονοκέφαλο. Δυσπεψία
	poh-noh-kef'-al-oh. this-pep-see'-a
Toothache. Diarrhoea	Πονόδοντο. Διάρροια
	poh-noth'-on-doh. the-ah'-re-ah
I have been sunburnt	Ἔχω ἐγκαύματα ἡλίου
	eh'-Ho en-gahv'-mat-a ill-ee'-oo
My feet are blistered	Τά πόδια μου ἐγέμισαν φουσκαλίδες
	tah poth'-e-ah-moo eh-yem'-iss-ahn foos-kah-lee'-thess
I want something for insect bites	θέλω κάτι γιά τά δαγκώματα τῶν ἐντόμων
	thel'-o kah'-te yah tah than-gom'-ah-tah ton en-dom'-on
I think it is poisoned	Νομίζω ὅτι ἔχει δηλητηριασθῆ (κακοφορμίση)
	noh-mee'-zoh ot'-ee eh'-He the-le-te-re-ahs-thee' (kah-koh-form-iss'-e)
I have a head cold	ἔχω κατάρρουν (συνάχι)
	eh'-Ho kat-arr'-oon (se-naH'-e)
My throat is very sore	ἔχω τρομερό πονόλαιμο
	eh'-Ho trom-air-oh' poh-nol'-em-on

HAIRDRESSERS

appointment (τό) ραντεβού, (ή) συνάντησις
    ran-day-voo', se-nan'-de-siss

bleach ξάνοιγμα μαλλιῶν *ksan'-eegh-mah mahl-yon'*

brush βούρτσα μαλλιῶν *voort-sah mahl-yon'*

colour rinse (ξέπλυμα βαφῆς *ksep'-le-mah vah-feese'*

comb (τό) χτένι, (ή) τσατσάρα *Hten'-e, tsah-tsah'-ra*

cut (τό) τραῦμα, (τό) κόψιμο *trahv'-ma, kop'-se-moh*

manicure (τό) μανικιούρ *man-e-cure'*

perm (τό) περμανάντ *pair-ma-nant'*

set (τό) τύλιγμα, μιζανπλί
    tee'-leegh-mah, meez-ahm-plee'

shampoo (τό) σαμπουάν *sahm-poo-ahn'*

tint (ή) βαφή *vah-fee'*

May I make an appointment? Μπορεῖτε νά μοῦ ὁρίσετε
    ἕνα ραντεβού;
    boh-ree'-teh na moo or-ees'-et-eh en'-nah ran-day-voo'

I want a shave ξύρισμα παρακαλῶ
    ksee'-rees-ma pah-rah-kah-lo'

I want a haircut κόψιμο μαλλιῶν, παρα-
    καλῶ
    kop'-se-moh mal-yon', pah-rah-kah-lo'

Not too short ὄχι πολύ κοντά
    oh'-He pol-'le kon-dah'

I would like it short κοντά, παρακαλῶ
    kon-dah', pah-rah-kah-lo'

I want a shampoo and set θέλω λούσιμο καί μιζανπλί
    thel'-o loo'-se-moh kay meez-ahm-plee'

It is too hot (cold) εἶναι πολύ ζεστό (κρύο)
    ee'-neh pol-lee' zes-toh' (kree'-oh)

It is not dry   δέν ἔχουν στεγνώσει
      then eh'-Hoon stegh-noss'-e
That is excellent   θαυμάσια
      thav-mahss'-e-a

THE PHOTOGRAPHIC SHOP

black and white film (τό) ἀχρώματο φίλμ
      aH-ro'-ma-toh film
camera (ἡ) φωτογραφική μηχανή
      fo-to-ghraf-e-kee' miH-an-ee'
colour film (τό) ἔγχρωμο φίλμ *en'-Hroh-moh film*
develop ἐμφανίζω *em-fa-nee'-zoh*
enlarge μεγεθύνω *may-yeh-thee'-noh*
enlargement (ἡ) μεγέθυνσις *may-yeh'-theen-sis*
exposure-meter (τό) φωτόμετρον *fo-tom'-et-ron*
filter (τό) φίλτρο *feel'-tro*
glossy γυαλιστερό *yah-lees-teh-roh'*
lens (ὁ) φακός *fak-oss'*
lens-hood (τό) παρασολέϊγ *pah-rah-sol-ay'*
matt χρῶμα μουντό, μάτ *Hroh'-mah moon-doh'*, mat
negative (τό) ἀρνητικό *arr-ne-te-koh'*
print θετικό *that-e-koh'*
range-finder (τό) τηλέμετρον *tee-lem'-eh-tron*
shutter διάφραγμα *the-ah'-fragh-ma*
view-finder (τό) εἰκονοσκόπιον *ee-kon-os-skop'-e-on*
tripod (τό) τρίποδο *tree'-poth-oh*

Will you develop this film?   Μπορεῖτε νά μοῦ κάνετε τήν
      ἐμφάνησι αὐτοῦ τοῦ φίλμ;
      boh-ree'-teh nah moo kah'-net-eh tin em-fahn'-e-se
      af-too' too film

I would like some prints (enlargements)	Θά ἤθελα μερικά φωτογραφικά ἀντίτυπα (μεριυες μεγεθύνσεις)

thah ee'-thel-ah meh-re-kah' fo-to-ghraf-e-ka'
ahn-dee'-te-pa (meh-re-kess' meh-yeh-thin'-sees)

When will they be ready?	Πότε θά εἶναι ἔτοιμα;

poh'-teh thah ee'-neh et'-e-ma

There is something wrong with my camera	Κάτι ἔχει πάθει ἡ φωτογραφική μου μηχανή

kah'-te eh'-He pah'-the ee fo-to-ghraf-e-kee' moo me-Han-ee'

The film won't turn	Τό ρουλό τοῦ φίλμ δέν γυρίζει

toh roo-loh' too film then ye-ree'-ze

OTHER SHOPS

baker ἀρτοπωλεῖον *ar-top-oh-lee'-on*
butcher κρεοπωλεῖον *kreh-oh-pol-ee'-on*
cake shop ζαχαροπλαστεῖον *zaH-ah-roh-plas-tee'-on*
cleaner καθαριστήριον *kah-thah-re-steer'-e-on*
confectioner ζαχαροπλαστεῖον *zach-ah-roh-plas-tee'-on*
dairy γαλακτοπωλεῖον *ghah-lak-toh-pol-ee'-on*
draper ἐμπορικό κατάστημα
      em-bor-e-koh' kat-ahs'-te-mah
fishmonger ἰχθυοπωλεῖον *iH-the-op-ol-ee'-on*
fruiterer ὀπωροπωλεῖον, μανάβικο
      op-oh-rop-oh-lee'-on, mahn-av'-e-koh
grocer παντοπωλεῖον *pan-doh-pol-ee'-on*
ironmonger σιδεροπωλεῖον *see-there-oh-pol-ee'-on*
jeweller κοσμηματοπωλεῖον *kos-me-ma-toh-pol-ee'-on*
newsagent ἐφημεριδοπωλεῖον *effy-merry-thop-ol-e e'-on*

perfumery μυροπωλεῖον *me-rop-ol-ee'-on*
shoe repairer μπαλωματῆς, τσαγκάρης
              bal-om-ah-tees', tsang-ah'-rees
shoe shop ὑποδηματοποιεῖον *e-poth-e-ma-toh-pee'-on*
stationer χαρτοπωλεῖον *Har-top-ol-ee'-on*

Festivals, Folklore and Entertainment

There are many Greek religious festivals, particularly
at Easter time when there are sacred candlelight processions, feasting and drama—the three weeks of carnival
before Lent is one of the most festive times of the year.
Easter itself is the principal feast of the Orthodox Church;
after a day of mourning on Good Friday, the processions
begin to wind their way around the streets, and on
Saturday morning the funereal atmosphere begins to
break up while remaining thoroughly reverent. At the
midnight services on Easter Day the full glory of massed
candlepower lights up the churches, and there is a
wonderful feeling of jubilation which continues all day
long as the celebrations really get under way. Probably no
other Christian Church puts so much joy and fervour into
the Resurrection as do the Greeks.

The Athens Festival is held from mid-July to mid-
September, when world-famous foreign companies and
performers present symphony concerts, classical master-
pieces of the theatre and opera, and ballet. The out-
standing feature of the Festival programme is the cycle of
ancient tragedies and comedies by Aeschylus, Sophocles,

Euripides and Aristophanes, performed by the National Theatre of Greece. Most events are staged in the open-air theatre of Herodes Atticus which has stood at the foot of the Acropolis since 160 AD. Another event well worth seeing is the "Son et Lumière" classical pageant, held every summer on the slopes of the Acropolis.

To meet the Athenians in gayer mood, visit the annual Wine Festival at Daphni—about 5 miles from the centre of Athens. During the 15 days of the festival you may taste, free of charge, more than 60 varieties of mellow Greek wines, watch national dancing and enjoy the carefree atmosphere of the tavernas.

The great annual festival of Greece is held at Epidaurus, some 100 miles by road from Athens, for some weeks prior to the Athens Festival. In ancient times Aesculapius, the pagan god of medicine, had his shrine here and the Greek citizens came in their thousands to restore their health. The hot springs are still in use. The Epidaurus Festival was inaugurated in 1954 and is now firmly established as an artistic institution. The National Theatre of Greece present the ancient dramas on Saturday and Sunday evenings, and the texts of the plays are translated into the main European languages. The theatre, which stands on the western slopes of Mount Kynortion, was discovered during excavations made between 1881 and 1928. It is one of the best-preserved of all ancient theatres, and was built in the 4th century BC. The orchestra is circular in shape and has a diameter of 22 yards; there are 55 tiers of stone seats (capacity 14,000), and the acoustics are so incredibly good that a stage whisper can be clearly heard in the back row.

Folklore

Many of the religious feasts, although Christian, have their origins in the ancient rites of the Greek tribes. Over the centuries the gods, nymphs and gorgons of mythology have become embodied in Christian saints and other spirits, while Alexander the Great lives on as the symbol of chivalry and the saviour of the weak. The folk dances and songs preserve a tradition which dates back to the days of ancient Greece, and the same dancing postures which you see portrayed on the earliest Greek vases are those very postures which the dancers recapture today.

The Greek Folk Dances and Songs Society gives performances of the various regional dances in colourful local costume. These are accompanied by song and music played on the lute, violin, clarinet, "lyra" and "santouri". The concerts are given every evening from June to September in the ancient theatre at Piraeus.

Remember to check dates and times of performances, which may be altered at the last minute; this applies to any festival or folklore event (a list of which can be had from the Greek National Tourist Office in London), and the Tourist Information Office in Athens—6 Karagheorgi Servais Street—will be able to check for you.

Entertainment

The more modern world of show business has developed to a great extent in recent years, particularly in the Athens area. Here alone there are some 40 cinemas, some of which are open-air. There are two seasons for theatres and cinemas in Greece; from October to April or May (depending on the weather), and from May or June to the end of September. In Athens there are 12 summer and 15 winter theatres. Revues are also popular, and numerous dance halls and night clubs offer a wide variety of entertainment from the latest "pop" music on a juke-box to first-class floor shows given by visiting artistes.

Sport, The Beach

It is hardly surprising that the country which gave us the Olympic Games should today provide facilities for every kind of sport. In and around Athens the visitor will find all the sporting amenities he could require—tennis courts, golf courses, rifle ranges, gymnasiums, fencing schools, riding, rowing and yachting clubs, swimming pools, and so on. Soccer, track and field athletics attract the largest crowds, and basket ball has become very popular. Matches generally take place every Sunday afternoon. The Hellenic Automobile and Touring Club organise the Acropolis Rally at the end of May, and a shorter rally is held in November.

Yachting is well catered for, there being some 100 permanent supply bases that are marked by a blue and yellow stripped section of quayside. Full-scale marinas are now being built, and the formalities for visiting yachtsmen under foreign flags have been simplified. All vessels are issued with a "transit log" at the first port of call; this should be shown at any further ports visited, and it is completed and kept by the authorities at the final port of call.

Fishermen will find the Greek waters a happy hunting ground; no permit is necessary unless you want to do underwater fishing. In the wonderfully clear water that is a feature of the Aegean, this can be most enjoyable—photographs can be taken at a depth of 80 feet without artificial light. For further information apply to the Greek Amateur Fishing and Underwater Activities Federation, 3 Stadium Street, Athens.

Game shooting is a favourite sport, there being over 350 clubs throughout the country. The close season is generally between 16th March and 24th August. There is no limit to the size of your "bag", and information regarding the necessary permits and licence should be obtained from the National Tourist Organisation.

Mountaineering, in this country of mountains, is gaining in popularity, and useful addresses are: Greek Touring Club (mainly an excursion club with a small mountaineering section), 21 Amalia Avenue, Athens; Greek Mountaineering Club (exclusive activities are climbing and skiing), 7 Karagheorghi Street, Athens; Federation of Greek Excursion Clubs, 4 Dragatsaniou Street, Athens.

Finally, the beaches. Of these there are plenty; those in the north are less populated than the Attic beaches near Athens, and are just as fine. Many are broken by rocky outcrops, from which it is quite safe to bathe. Some form of footwear is advisable, for if the scorching sand does not hurt your feet then the sea-urchins might well do so.

USEFUL WORDS AND PHRASES
bathe κολυμπῶ *koh-lim-boh'*

bathing cabin (ή) καμπίνα *kah-bee'-nah*
bathing cap (ή) σκούφια μπάνιου *skoo'-fe-ah bahn'-you*
bathing costume μπανιερό, μαγιώ *bahn-yah-roh', my-yoh'*
bay (ό) ὅρμος *orr'-moss*
beach (ή) παραλία *pah-rah-lee'-ah*
boat (ή) βάρκα *var'-kah*
buoy (ή) σημαδούρα *se-mah-thoo'-rah*
canoe (τό) κανώ *kah-noh'*
cliff ἀπότομος βράχος *ah-poh'-tom-oss vraH'-oss*
coast (ή) ἀκτή *ak-tee'*
current (τό) ρεῦμα *rrev'-mah*
deck chair (ή) πολυθρόνα καταστρώματος
      pol-e-thron'-a kat-as-trom'-a-toss
diving board (ή) κολυμβητική ἐξέδρα
      kol-eem-ve-te-kee' ex-eth'-ra
fish ψαρεύω *psa-rev'-o*
fish (v.) ψάρι *psa'-re*
slippers παντόφλες *pan-doff'-less*
jelly-fish μέδουσα, τσούχτρα *meth'-oo-sa, tsooH'-tra*
pebbles χαλίκια, χοχλάκια *Ha-leek'-ya, HoH-lak'-ya*
raft σχεδία, πλῶτα *sHeth-ee'-a, plot'-a*
rocks βράχοι, βράχια *vrah'-He, vrah'-H'ya*
sand (ή) ἄμμος *ahm'-os*
sandhills (ή) ἀμμουδιά *ahm-oo-the-a'*
shell (τό) ὄστρακον *os'-tra-kon*
snorkel ἀεροσωλήν δύτου *ah-air-o-so-leen' thee'-too*
sunshade ἀλεξήλιον, παρασόλι
      alex-ee'-le-on, pa-ra-sol'-e
tide (ή) παλίρροια *pa-leer'-re-ah*
water skis (τό) θαλάσσιο σκί *thal-ass'-e-o ske*
wave (τό) κῦμα *kee'-ma*

F   81

Which is the way to the beach?	Ποῦ εἶναι ὁ δρόμος γιά τήν Παραλία;
	poo ee'-neh oh throm'-oss yah tin pah-rah-lee'-ah
Can I hire a deck-chair (sunshade, cabin)	Μπορῶ νά νοικιάσω πολυθρόνα-καταστρώμα-τος, (παρασόλι, καμπίνα)
	boh-roh' na nik-e-ahss'-o poll-e-thron'-ah kat-as-trom'-a-tos (pah-rah-sol'-e, kah-been'-ah)
Can I hire some flippers?	Μπορῶ νά νοικιάσω κο-λυμβητικά πτερύγια;
	boh-roh' na nik-e-ahss'-o kol-eem-ve-te-kah' ptair-ee'-yah
Can I hire a snorkel?	Μπορῶ νά νοικιάσω ἀναπ-νευστικό σωλῆνα;
	boh-roh' na nik-e-ahss'-o ah-nahp-nef-ste-koh' sol-ee'-na
Where is it safe to bathe?	Ποῦ μπορεῖ νά κολυμβήση κανείς μέ ἀσφάλεια; (χωρίς κίνδυνο);
	poo voh-ree' na kol-eem-vee'-se kan-ees' meh ahs-fahl'-yah (Hor-ees' kin'-the-no)
Can I go fishing?	Μπορῶ νά ψαρέψω;
	boh-roh' na psah-rep'-so
I am not a good swimmer	Δέν εἶμαι καλός κολυμ-βητής
	then ee'-meh kah-loss' kol-eem-ve-tees'
Bathing prohibited	Ἀπαγορεύεται τό κολύμ-βημα (τό κολύμπι)
	ah-pah-gho-rev'-eh-teh toh kol-eem'-ve-ma (toh kol-eem'-be)
I only want to sunbathe	θέλω νά κάνω ἡλιοθεραπεία
	thel'-oh na ka'-no ee-le-o-ther-a-pee'-a

Can I hire a sailing boat (rowing, motor boat)?	Μπορῶ νά νοικιάσω βάρκα μέ πανί (μέ κουπιά, μέ βενζινάκατο);

boh-roh' na nik-e-ahss'-o var'-ka meh pahn-ee'
(meh koo-pe-ah', meh ven-ze-na'-ka-to)

Where can I go water-skiing?	Ποῦ μπορῶ νά πάγω γιά θαλάσσιο σκί;

poo boh-roh' na pa'-ghoh yah tha-lass'-e-o ski

Is it dangerous?	εἶναι ἐπικίνδυνο;

ee'-neh eppy-kin'-the-noh

Are there any rocks there?	ὑπάρχουν βράχοι ἐκεῖ;

ee-parr'-Hoon vrah'-He ek-kee'

Does it shelve quickly?	βαθαίνει ἀπότομα;

va-then'-e ah-pot'-om-a

Is there a shower?	ὑπάρχει ἐδῶ ντούς;

ee-parr'-He eth-oh' dooce

Post Office, Telephones

The Central Post Office in Athens is in Costa Kotzias Square, and there is a large branch office on the corner of Karagheorghi and Nikis Streets, near Constitution (Syntagma) Square. Other branch offices are in all areas of the city; blue and white mail boxes for posting letters are located in main streets, outside banks and principal hotels. The hotel manager will usually undertake to post your mail, and stamps can be obtained either at the hotel, from post offices, or from kiosks on the pavements.

Telegrams and telephones are the responsibility of the Telecommunications Organisation of Greece (O.T.E.), not of the Post Office. Public call-boxes are few in number, but you can always make local calls from a kiosk or shop. The public boxes work on the "jeton" principle; in exchange for your drachma the kiosk attendant will give you a metal counter (a *kerma*) which you then feed to the box. If you get into difficulties, dial 13 for help.

USEFUL WORDS AND PHRASES

cablegram διεθνές τηλεγράφημα
      the-eth-ness' tee-lay-ghraf'-e-ma

call (τό) τηλεφώνημα *tee-lay-fon'-e-ma*

collection (ή) συλλογή *se-logh-ee'*

directory (ό) κατάλογος διευθύνσεων
      ka-ta'-lo-ghos the-ef-thin'-seh-on

international money order διεθνής ἐπιταγή
      the-eth-nees' ep-e-tagh-ee'

letter (τό) γράμμα *gram'-ma*

letter box (τό) γραμματοκιβώτιον
      ghram-ma-tok-e-vot'-e-on

post card (ή) κάρτα *kar'-ta*

post office (τό) ταχυδρομεῖον *tah-He-thro-mee'-on*

postal order (ή) ταχυδρομική ἐπιταγή
      tah-He-thro-me-kee' ep-e-ta-yee'

number (ό) ἀριθμός *arith-moss'*

register συστημένο *sis-tim-men'-o*

stamp (τό) γραμματόσημο *ghram-ma-toss'-e-mo*

telegram (τό) τηλεγράφημα *tee-lay-ghraf'-e-ma*

telephone (τὸ) τηλέφωνο *tee-lef'-on-o*

to telephone τηλεφωνῶ *tee-lef-on-oh'*

telephone box (ό) τηλεφωνικός θάλαμος
      tee-lef-on-e-koss' tha'-la-moss

Where is the nearest post office?	ποῦ εἶναι τό πλησιέστερο ταχυδρομεῖο;

poo ee'-neh toh plee-se-est'-air-o tah-He-thro-mee'-o

I want to send this post card (letter, parcel)	Θέλω νά στείλω αὐτή τήν κάρτα (αὐτό τό γράμμα, αὐτό τό δέμα)

thel'-oh na stee'-loh af-tee' tin kar'-ta (af-toh' toh ghram'-ma, af-toh' toh them'-ah)

I want to register this letter	Θέλω νά στείλω αὐτό τό γράμμα συστημένο

thel'-oh nah stee'-loh af-toh' toh ghram'-ma see-ste-men'-o

Are there any letters for me?	Ἦλθε κανένα γράμμα γιά μένα;

eel'-theh kah-nen'-ah ghram'-ma yah men'-ah

Is there a parcel for me?	Ἐλάβατε κανένα δέμα γιά μένα;

eh-lahv'-ah-teh kah-nen'-ah them'-ah yah men'-ah

Here is my passport	Ἰδού τό διαβατήριό μου

ee-thoo' toh the-a-va-tee'-re-oh'-moo

Medical Services

Any medical, dental or hospital services must be paid for as there are no reciprocal arrangements between Greece and Great Britain. You are therefore strongly advised to take out an insurance policy through your travel agent to cover you against the possibility of such treatment. It costs between 50p and £1 to cover a 17-day holiday period.

USEFUL WORDS AND PHRASES
accident (τό) δυστύχημα *the-stee'-Him-a*
ambulance (τό) ἀσθενοφόρον *ass-then-o-for'-on*
appendicitis (ἡ) σκωληκοειδίτις *sko-le-ko-e-thee'-tis*
bandage (ὁ) ἐπίδεσμος *ep-ee'-thez-moss*
bite (τό) δάγκωμα *thah'-go-ma*
blister (ἡ) φουσκαλίδα *foo-ska-lee'-tha*
burn (τό) ἔγκαυμα *en'-gahv-ma*
chill (τό) κρυολόγημα *kre-o-loy'-e-ma*
constipation (ἡ) δυσκοιλιότης *this-kil-e-ott'-is*
cough (ὁ) βήχας *vee'-Has*
to cough βήχω *vee'-Ho*
cramp (ἡ) κράμπα *kram'-pa*
cut (τό) τραῦμα *trav'-ma*
dentist (ὁ) ὀδοντογιατρός *oth-on-doy-a-tross'*
diarrhoea (ἡ) διάρροια *the-ar'-re-a*
doctor (ὁ) γιατρός *yat-ross'*
faint (ἡ) λιποθυμία *le-poth-e-mee'-a*
fever (ὁ) πυρετός *peer-et-oss'*
fracture (τό) σπάσιμο *spass'-e-mo*
hospital (τό) νοσοκομεῖο *no-so-ko-mee'-o*
indigestion δυσπεψία *this-pep-see'-a*
influenza (ἡ) γρίππη *ghrip'-ee*
insomnia (ἡ) ἀϋπνία *eye-ip-nee'-a*
injection (ἡ) ἔνεσις *en'-es-iss*
nurse (ὁ, ἡ) νοσοκόμος *nos-o-kom'-oss*
pain (ὁ) πόνος *pon'-oss*
poison (τό) δηλητήριον *thee-le-teer'-e-on*
policeman (in big cities) (ὁ) ἀστυφύλακας *ass-te-feel'-ak-ass*
(in other towns) χωροφύλακας *hor-o-feel'-ak-ass*

sling (ὁ) ἐπίδεσμος ἐκ τοῦ ὤμου
  ep-pee'-thez-moss ek too om'-oo
splint (ὁ) νάρθηκας *nar'-the-kass*
sprain (τό) στραμπούλιγμα *stram-boo'-ligh-mah*
sting (τό) κέντρισμα *ken'-driz-ma*
stomach ache (ὁ) πονόκοιλος *poh-nok'-e-loss*
sunstroke (ἡ) ἡλίασις *il-ee'-a-siss*
surgery κλινική *kle'-ne-kee'*
temperature (ἡ) θερμοκρασία *ther-mo-kra-see'-a*
throat (ὁ) λαιμός *lem-oss'*
toothache (ὁ) πονόδοντος *pon-oth'-on-doss*
to vomit κάνω ἐμετό *ka'-no em-et-oh'*
vomit (*n.*) (ὁ) ἐμετός *em-et-oss'*

Call an ambulance quickly   Καλέσετε γρήγορα τό ἀσ-
                                  θενοφόρον
  kal-ess'-eh-teh ghree'-ghor-ah toh ahs-then-o-for'-on
Call a policeman quickly   Καλέσετε γρήγορα ἕναν
                                  ἀστυφύλακα
  kal-ess'-eh-teh ghree'-ghor-ah en'-nan ahs-te-feel'-a-ka
Stand back   Παραμερίσατε παρακαλῶ
  pah-rah-meh-ree'-sah-teh pah-rah-kah-lo'
Give him (her) air   Κάνετέ του (της) λίγο ἀέρα
  kan-eh-teh'-too (-tiss) lee'-ghoh ah-air'-ah
Do not move him (her)   Μήν τόν (τήν) μετακινή-
                                  σετε
  min ton (tin) met-ah-ke-nee'-set-eh
Is there a doctor near here? Ὑπάρχει γιατρός ἐδῶ
                                  κοντά;
  ee-parr'-He yah-tross' eh-thoh' kon-da'

Have you a bandage?)Εχετε κανένα ἐπίδεσμο;
eh'-Heh-te kan-en'-a ep-pee'-thes-moh

I have a pain here Πονῶ ἐδῶ
poh-noh' eh-thoh'

Bring some hot (cold) water Φέρετε λίγο ζεστό (κρύο) νερό
fair'-et-eh lee'-ghoh zest-oh' (kree'-oh) neh-roh'

Bring me a blanket Φέρετέ μου μία κουβέρτα
fair'-et-eh-moo mee'-a koo-vair'-ta

I am feeling very ill Αἰσθάνομαι πολύ ἄσχημα
ess-than'-o-meh pol-lee' ahs'-He-ma

Please bring a doctor Καλέσετε τόν γιατρό, παρακαλῶ
ka-less'-et-eh ton yah-troh', pa-ra-ka-loh'

Do you have any pain here? Πονᾶτε ἐδῶ;
poh-na'-teh eh-thoh'

Where is the nearest dentist? Ποῦ εἶναι ὁ πλησιέστερος ὀδοντογιατρός;
poo ee'-neh o plee-se-ess'-tair-oss oh-thon-doh-yah-tross'

Will you give me an injection? Θέλω νά μοῦ κάνετε μία ἔνεσι
thel'-oh na moo kan'-et-eh mee'-a en-ess'-ee

Useful Information

Banks, Currency

Banks are well organised and there is no language problem. Have your passport handy in order to avoid any delay. Hours of business are from 9 am to 1 pm, Sundays and holidays excepted, though for the benefit of tourists some banks reopen for certain hours in the afternoon.

The basic unit of currency is the drachma, which is split into 100 lepta. No more than 750 drachmas may be brought into the country, in bank notes of 50 and 100 dr. only; the same amount may be taken out without declaration provided that your stay has not exceeded two months.

Insert below the prevailing rate of exchange, as this is subject to fluctuation:

1 drachma (coin) =	30 drachmas (coin) =
2 drachmas (coin) =	50 drachmas (note) =
5 drachmas (coin) =	100 drachmas (note) =
10 drachmas (coin) =	1000 drachmas (note) =
20 drachmas (coin) =	

Coins are also issued for 10, 20 and 50 lepta, and you will probably hear street traders call the various coins and notes by familiar names, which can be rather confusing.

Tipping

A service charge is included in most bills, but it is customary to give an additional small tip (5% or so) to the waiter, or a few drachmas to the pot boy in the taverna.

Annual Holidays

Shops, banks etc., are closed on Christmas Day and Boxing Day, New Year's Day, Epiphany (6th January), Independence Day (25th March), the Monday following the end of Carnival and the beginning of Lent, Good Friday, Easter Monday, the Feast of SS. Constantine and

Helen (the King's name-day, 21st May), the Feast of the
Holy Spirit (6th June), the Feast of the Holy Virgin
(August 15th), and "Ochi" Day (commemorating
Greece's entry into the war on the side of the Allies, after
being attacked by Italy on the 28th October 1940).

Tobacconists' Kiosks

Called *Periptero*, these are liberally situated along
the streets and sell not only Greek and imported cigarettes
but also sweets, aspirins, cosmetics, pencils, postcards,
razor blades, stationery, imitation jewellery and a variety
of other useful articles. Those in the centre of Athens
have foreign newspapers and magazines. *Peripteros* also
serve as unofficial taxi-ranks and information centres.

Public Conveniences

Usually situated in the town or village square, these
are fairly obvious if not particularly inviting. In Athens
they are harder to find, but you may always use the
facilities provided by cafes and restaurants without
actually having to buy anything.

May I use your lavatory, please?	Μπορῶ νά χρησιμοποιήσω τήν τουαλέτα σας;
	boh-roh' nah Hree-see-mo-pe-ee'-so tin too-ah-let'-ah sahs

Tourist Police

The tourist police are available day and night to
provide tourists with information and also to deal with
complaints. They speak foreign languages, and have
power to arrest any persons annoying or exploiting

tourists and to enforce all regulations governing hotels, travel agencies, archaeological sites, guides, beaches and so on.

British and Continental Clothing Sizes

Dresses and suits (Women)   *(Junior Miss)*

British	34	36	38	40	42	44	32	33	35	36	38	39
Continental	40	42	44	46	48	50	38	40	42	44	46	48

Men's suits and overcoats

British	36	38	40	42	44	46
Continental	46	48	50	52	54	56

Shirts and collars

British	14	14½	15	15½	16	16½	17
Continental	36	37	38	39	41	42	43

Shoes

British	3	4	5	6	7	8	9	10	11	12
Continental	36	37	38	39	41	42	43	44	46	47

Hats

British	6½	6⅝	6¾	6⅞	7	7⅛	7¼	7⅜	7½
Continental	53	54	55	56	57	58	59	60	61

Stockings

British	8	8½	9	9½	10	10½
Continental	0	1	2	3	4	5

Socks

British	9½	10	10½	11	11½
Continental	38–39	39–40	40–41	41–42	42–43

Gloves are the same size as in Britain.

Electric Current

In Athens and most of the mainland this is 220 volts A.C., but in some places, mainly the islands, it is 110 volts D.C., so your shaver (and other appliances) will need an adaptor.

Conversion Tables

DISTANCES

Distances are marked in kilometres. To convert kilometres to miles, divide the km. by 8 and multiply by 5. Convert miles to km. by dividing the miles by 5 and multiplying by 8. A mile is 1 km. 610 m.

km.	miles or *km.*	miles	km.	miles or km.	miles
1·6	1	0·6	16·1	10	6·2
3·2	2	1·2	32·2	20	12·4
4·8	3	1·9	48·3	30	18·6
6·4	4	2·5	64·4	40	24·9
8·1	5	3·1	80·5	50	31·1
9·7	6	3·7	160·9	100	62·1
11·3	7	4·4	321·9	200	124·2
12·9	8	5·0	804·7	500	310·7
14·5	9	5·6	1609·4	1000	621·4

Other units of length

1 centimetre	= 0·39 in.	1 inch = 25·4 millimetres
1 metre	= 39·37 in.	1 foot = 0·30 metre (30 cm.)
10 metres	= 32·81 ft.	1 yard = 0·91 metre

WEIGHTS

The unit you will come into most contact with is the kilogram, or kilo. To convert kg. to lbs., multiply by 2 and add $\frac{1}{10}$ of the result. One kilo (1000 gr.) is 2 lb. 3 oz.; one stone is 6·35 kg.; one cwt. is 51 kg.

grams	ounces		ounces	grams
50	1·75		1	28.0
100	3·50		2	57·1
250	8·80		4	114·3
500	17·6		8	228·6

kg.	lbs. or kg.	lbs.	kg.	lbs. or kg.	lbs.
0·5	1	2·2	3·6	8	17·6
0·9	2	4·4	4·1	9	19·8
1·4	3	6·6	4·5	10	22·1
1·8	4	8·8	9·1	20	44·1
2·3	5	11·0	11·3	25	55·1
2·7	6	13·2	22·7	50	110·2
3·2	7	15·4	45·4	100	220·5

LIQUIDS

Petrol being sold in litres, the following table (in Imperial gallons) will aid your calculations—remember that while an Imperial gallon is roughly $4\frac{1}{2}$ litres, an American gallon is only 3.8 litres. One litre is about $1\frac{3}{4}$ pints, a pint is 0·57 litre.

litres	gals. *or* l.	gals.	litres	gals. *or* l.	gals.
4·6	1	0·2	36·4	8	1·8
9·1	2	0·4	40·9	9	2·0
13·6	3	0·7	45·5	10	2·2
18·2	4	0·9	90·9	20	4·4
22·7	5	1·1	136·4	30	6·6
27·3	6	1·3	181·8	40	8·8
31·8	7	1·5	227·3	50	11·0

TYRE PRESSURES

lbs. per sq. inch	17	18	19	20
kg. per sq. cm.	1k 200	1k 250	1k 350	1k 400

lbs. per sq. inch	21	22	23	24
kg. per sq. cm.	1k 475	1k 500	1k 600	1k 700

lbs. per sq. inch	25	26	27	28
kg. per sq. cm.	1k 750	1k 850	1k 900	1k 950

THREE MONTHS (*Self-Tuition*) BOOKS

Why not learn the language properly in time for next year's holiday? Hugo's "Three Months" series includes Portuguese, Dutch, Norwegian, Danish and Swedish as well as more popular languages such as French, German, Spanish and Italian, and is just right for absolute beginners. Essentially practical, each book has our unique, easy-to-read imitated pronunciation.

HUGOPHONE RECORDS *for pronunciation*

Don't be put off talking to people in their own language by thinking how funny you will sound, but break the "sound barrier"—that unconscious resistance to perfect pronunciation—with a Hugophone record. This will increase your confidence and greatly improve your pronunciation. One 12″ L.P. per language has five conversations on travel subjects, spoken slowly at first and then at normal speech rate. Text-cards are also provided. The series covers French, German, Spanish, Italian, Russian, and English for foreign students.

POCKET DICTIONARIES

A Hugo dictionary is a very useful "extra" on your holiday abroad. In so many cases the translation or use of only one word will solve a difficulty or render a more complicated phrase unnecessary. Over 22,000 headwords in each language—French, German, Spanish, Italian and Dutch—all with imitated pronunciation, make these two-way dictionaries invaluable for both tourists and businessmen. The Russian dictionary is 32 pages longer. There is also an all-English dictionary, with about 25,000 entries in 640 pages.

Full details of all Hugo publications will be sent upon request.